Life Wins!

A Collection of Essays and Sermons

by

Dr. Eugene R. "Woody" Widrick

Edited by Alex N. Beavers, Jr., and Linda W. Beavers

ISBN 978-0-615-38362-0

All Rights Reserved

Copyright 2010

Palma Sola Publishing

Table of Contents

Foreword 1
The Author 3
The Editors 4
Life Wins 5
Marginalia 8
To Outgrow The Past 12
God as Mother, Mother as God 15
Maundy Thursday 19
Not the Dream but the Reality of Life 21
Lent 26
Living the Spiritual Life: Letting Go 30
Bound in the Bundle of Life 34
Christmas Eve 37
Who is Jesus 39
Little Saint and the Smell of Flowers 43
Time Like An Ever Flowing Stream 47
On Letting the Bears Rejoice 51
Why You Should Give Money to the FRS, and How Much ... 55
The Goodness of Life and Death 59
An Incident In The Life Of Three Little Pigs And One Big Bad Wolf ... 61
Waiting For 63
Gratitude 67
The Crisis 69
System or Special Creation 73
The Earth as Nigger 76
On Being Shrunk 79
Belfort, New York, The Place Of My Dreams 83
Bibliography 94

Foreword

The Reverend Eugene R. "Woody" Widrick is a man that we have known for more than 25 years. When we first moved to the small community of Carlisle, Massachusetts in 1984, he was the relatively new minister at the Unitarian Universalist Church. Carlisle was then and still is a small town. Once many decades ago a farming community, it is now a suburb of Boston that has maintained a bit of its rural character with two acre minimum lot sizes and a group of citizens dedicated to keeping Carlisle as leafy as possible. The town has grown over the last 25 years from about 3,000 to about 6,000 residents, 3 churches, two real estate offices, one little shop selling essentials (milk, colas, snacks, fruit, etc.), a fire station, a police station, a library, and a school (elementary to middle school). One of the redeeming aspects of Carlisle was that even though the town was a 30 minute drive to Boston, the nearest strip mall was 6 miles away from town center.

Although we were raised in the Protestant faiths (Methodist and Presbyterian), after trying several of the local churches, we decided that this soft spoken man of slight stature that was the preacher at the Unitarian Church was the person that we wanted to listen to and talk with on Sunday mornings. The Unitarian Church doctrine was a wee bit more flexible in its view of religious dogma than what we had experienced throughout our lives of having been raised mostly in the South. For starters, many Unitarians considered the Bible one of several "good" examples of religious literature. One of my Unitarian friends used to remark that Unitarians were often quiet during the singing of hymns because we were reading ahead to see if we agreed with the lyrics.

However, at that time and in that place, we found that the little old white clapboard UU church on the hill in Carlisle Center was the place for our family because of Woody Widrick. Woody is a person who in a few words could ask a brain freezing question, give you three things to mull over related to the question, plant a thought to live by while you were mulling over the three things, and then leave you feeling better for having heard what he had to say. And all of this was done in a soft voice that always had a hint that something either whimsical or profound was about to be said so you had better listen.

Over the years, even after we moved away from Carlisle, we have asked Woody to preside over the weddings of our children and the baptisms of our grandchildren. We also asked Woody to publish some of his sermons and thoughts so that other people could get the benefit of his insight into how thoughtful people could lead a spiritual life.

Finally he agreed, and we volunteered to help bring his thoughts to a broader audience. In the following are a few of Woody's sermons and essays for people to read, mull over, and think about. We are sure that you will find something here which will add to your life's spiritual substance.

Linda and Alex Beavers

The Author

Eugene R. (Woody) Widrick is Minister Emeritus of the First Religious Society of Carlisle, Massachusetts after having served as Head Minister for 24 years. He is a graduate of SUNY, Albany, New York (M.S.L.S.), Tufts University (B.D.) and Andover Newton Theological School (D. Min.). In addition to Carlisle, he and his wife of over 40 years, Trudi, have ministered at churches in Connecticut, New Hampshire, and Massachusetts. From 1968 to 1971, Woody and his family served at the Unitarian Church in Cape Town, South Africa.

The Editors

Linda W. Beavers has served in professional communication and leadership capacities for over 40 years in addition to being a dedicated mother of four and wife of one (her co-editor). During her career, she has worked for ExxonMobil, NASA, University of Houston, and Montgomery County Community College. During her days in Carlisle, among other things she was a reporter for the Carlisle Mosquito Newspaper covering the School Board as well serving as the President of the Red Balloon Co-op Nursery School. Linda is currently editor of the Mid-Peninsula Newcomers Club Newsletter based in Menlo Park, California. Linda is a graduate of the University of Massachusetts (Salem) with a B.S. in business education.

Alex N. Beavers, Jr. has been an executive in high tech industries for most of his career for companies such as General Electric, Schlumberger, Thomson Industries, and SRI International. He also was a managing partner in the consulting operations for PricewaterhouseCoopers. Alex is a graduate of Vanderbilt University (B.S.E.E.), University of Houston (M.S.E.E., Ph.D. E.E.) and Boston University (M.B.A.). He has several technical journal publications as well as numerous articles published in industry monthlies.

Life Wins

I sent an email to a friend and colleague of mine named Dawn telling her I was giving the sermon here today, and asked her "What should I say about Easter?"

She replied, "Life Wins." Her whole email was actually four words. "Life Wins. Love, Dawn." Discussing this with another friend we decided it could be the whole sermon: "Life wins. Love, Dawn." Rather like the speech Sir Winston Churchill gave to Harrow School in 1941 (Churchill, 2003). Churchill, famous during WW II as Prime Minister of the United Kingdom, had gone to Harrow School, a private boys' school, and he had been invited to address the student body. He got up and said "Never give in—never, never, never, in nothing great or small, large or petty, never give in except to convictions of honor and good sense. Never yield to force, never yield to the apparently overwhelming might of the enemy." And sat down. Enough said.

Life wins. But, we decided, people would expect more than two words, or four words, "Life wins. Love, Dawn." though sometimes brevity is better. So I will keep this short.

Easter comes around the arrival of Spring so we associate Easter with flowers and baby birds and the birth of animals – especially important when more of us lived in the country and on farms. Now about the only time we see lambs is in the supermarket wrapped in plastic film, but not so many years ago calves and lambs and colts and baby chicks would have been more familiar to all of us. Trudi and I lived for three years in Cape Town, South Africa, the Southern Hemisphere, and the seasons were reversed. Easter there was autumn, and Christmas came in the summer. Couldn't talk about "the flowers that bloom in the spring" for Easter and had to look at other meanings.

I think "Life Wins" pretty well sums up a lot of the other meanings. We live in a world where monetary wealth is pretty much the measure of value we turn to. Rich is good, poor is bad. We measure our lives pretty much by what we own – bombarded day and night on TV, radio, in print, signs, to buy, to have, to own. Dorothee Sölle, a German Lutheran theologian called this "Death by bread alone." (Sölle, Death by Bread Alone: Texts and Reflections on Religious Experience, 1978) "We do not live by bread alone," said Jesus, "but by every word that proceedeth out of the mouth of God." (*Matthew 4:4*) Death by bread alone, according to Sölle comes when we define ourselves by what we own, what our income is, and by our material wealth. We live in a world where GNP, Gross National Product, is used to measure the success or failure of countries. We invest in other countries based on their GNP. Bhutan, a small mountain kingdom between India and Tibet has been criticized for having a poorly growing economy. The King, Jigme Singye Wangchuck, in 1972 responded to the criticism by developing the concept of Gross National Happiness (GNH) (Wangchhuk, 2008). GNH was defined by the King as being based on Buddhist spiritual values as well as economic growth. GNP is based on economic growth, GNH is based on "the premise that true development of human society takes place when material and spiritual development occur side by side to complement and reinforce each other." The GNH is based on 7 measurements: Economic, Environmental, Physical, Mental, Workplace, Social, and Political wellness.

To date Bhutan has escaped the deforestation and strip mining that have occurred in other developing countries. Part of the reason, apparently, for unrest in Tibet is the strip mining and deforestation which is taking place under Chinese plans to raise the GNP of Tibet and China. Sacred ground for the Tibetans, GNP for the Chinese.

A recent survey of the perceived happiness of people found that the folks in Nigeria rank highest followed by Mexico (Bond, 2003). The United States ranked 16th and Britain 24th.

GNH is controversial, controversial because a lot of us are not so certain that spiritual values equal or trump economic values. Sölle wanted spiritual values to trump.

What are spiritual values? St. Paul in his letter to the Galatians (*Galatians 5:22-23*) defined them for us: Love, joy, peace, long suffering, gentleness, goodness, meekness, temperance.

The Boston Globe once contained an article about a study done in which employees of a company received $5,000 bonuses and were interviewed before and after they received the money about how happy they were (Goldberg, 2008). The finding was that the amount of perceived happiness related to receiving the money was in direct relationship to how much of the money was spent on other people or given to charity. Not the amount of the bonus even, but the percentage invested by the recipient in others.

P. T. Barnum (1810-1891) of Barnum and Bailey Circus fame, who is claimed to have said that "There is a sucker born every minute," was a Universalist and quite often took the pulpit in our churches. Barnum defined eternal life by saying "Eternal life is right life, here, there, everywhere." That is what we are talking about, living a right life, here, there, everywhere." Life here, life now, life today. Jesus taught us that. "Go, and sin no more" he says to the woman accused of immorality. Go live a right life. Isn't that the message for all of us? Live a right life.

Gerard Manly Hopkins, poet and priest and teacher, in one of his poems, "The Wreck of the Deutschland" (Hopkins, 1918) said "Let him easter in us, be a dayspring to the dimness of us, / be a crimson-cresseted east...." The message of Easter, whether we be humanist, deist, theist, Christian, heathen, or any other religious or philosophical position, is to take into ourselves the newness of life, to go and sin no more, to love our neighbors as ourselves, to live a right life, to know that no matter what else, life wins. And love.

March, 2008

Marginalia

We have been meeting here at the First Religious Building here in Carlisle, Massachusetts – or almost here – for 250 years. Actually 197 years on this spot and before that in a building to the right of where we are. If you check the Revolutionary War Monument out front, it is approximately where the front steps of the original building were located. That building was struck by lightning and burned in 1810, so this one was built. This building has gone through three major changes: In the middle 1800s the balcony was floored over to create this space and Union Hall below. In 1905 if I remember correctly, the whole building was jacked up high enough to add the ground floor, what some of would call the basement. The "new building" with space for a kitchen, elevator, classrooms, and offices was added in 1994.

There have been changes that were social, cultural, and spiritual. Our first settled minister, Paul Litchfield, died in 1828. Litchfield was an orthodox Christian, a Calvinist, and had resisted the ideas of Universalists and Unitarians for years. The calling of a minister to replace Litchfield turned into a conflict which split the congregation, eventually leading to the calling of a Universalist to this church and a substantial number of people going across the street to build a church with preaching and teaching more in line with the Calvinism of Litchfield. The Universalist was followed by a Unitarian minister.

Life is funny. Victor Carpenter and I have never worked together but I followed him in The Free Protestant (Unitarian) Church in Cape Town, South Africa going there in 1968. Now Vic has followed me here though there has been a six year gap. This church had a Harvard Divinity School student here as an intern from 1979 to 1981 named Eric Heller. Eric eventually ended up in South Africa where he preached on occasion at the Unitarian Church and earned a Doctor of Philosophy degree at the University of Stellenbosch in 1995. Eric's dissertation was on Unitarianism in South Africa. South African Unitarians – Free Protestants as they called themselves – were and are, according to Heller a "marginal" group, that is, people who live at the margins of society, are open to other ways of being – in the case of South Africa open to Non-White members, communicative with other religious groups. During the time Victor and I were in Cape Town there was a Parsi family, Zoroastrians from India, in the church. No one asked them to convert, no one objected when the woman taught Sunday school. The church did not require, as some groups did, that admission to the church or where people were seated be determined by racial classification. The church had Colored members and had had since its founding in 1865. The church was actively engaged in building relationships with other religious groups, Quaker, Bahai, Sufi, Islam. Building bridges between various elements of society

The concept of "marginal" as a description of human personality or groups was postulated in 1921 by Robert Ezra Park at the University of Chicago (Park, 1921). Park claimed that group solidarity correlates to a great extent to the animosity we have toward other groups. As we mix and fuse cultures, become "more civilized" in Park's terminology, people can find themselves on the margins of cultures where they can observe their own culture and other cultures with some detachment, learn to accept differences, develop appreciation, develop mature adjustments. Marginal people and groups build bridges across cultural divides, open paths of communication, and establish relationships.

Dr. Billie Davis in a speech delivered in 1997 to the National Honor Society in Psychology (Davis B. , 1997) spoke of marginality:

"What makes real people?" she started her talk:

"What makes real people?

"Before I was seven years old I asked my father that question. 'What's the matter with you?' my dad answered in response. 'What kind of notion is that—real people?'

'People that live in houses,' I tried to explain. 'People that stay together in towns.'

"I was expressing in a child's blunt language the basic questions of theology, philosophy, and psychology. What is human? How do people become what they are?"

She goes on to explain that she was born into a family of migrant farm laborers. "I heard people," she continues, "call us *gypsies, tramps, migrants, bums, farm labor, transients,* and *oakies.* The designations so obviously set us apart that I began to conceive of the townsfolk as real people. I asked 'what makes real people' because I had sensed the vital concepts of being and belonging. What does it mean to be a person? What does it mean to belong?"

What makes real people? Who is a person? Who are real people to us?

The Calvinism of the early Congregationalists, as preached in this church up to 1828 – to over simplify a bit, held that God was all powerful and all knowing, omnipotent and omniscient. Therefore God knew, before He created Heaven and Earth, everything that was going to happen, and had, in a sense, chosen who among us were to be saved and go to Heaven and who among us were damned to Hell. And, since God knew and knows all, there is nothing we can do to change it. We can hope to be among the elect—the saved—but we cannot know.

The Universalists believed that God had chosen for all souls to go to Heaven. The Unitarians believed that human beings could chose to be good, had elements of divinity within them, and were therefore worthy of salvation, could chose their own fate.. It was a conflict, in a sense, over who are real people? The Universalist answer was everyone goes to Heaven therefore everyone is a real person. The Unitarians believed in the "progressive capacity" of human beings; that we have within ourselves the ability to grow in holiness, knowledge and righteousness. If we had not earned Heaven we still can. In 1784 Charles Chauncey, minister of the First Church in Boston from 1727 to 1787, published a book, *The Mystery Hid From Ages and Generations,* which begins "As the First Cause of all things is infinitely benevolent, 'tis not easy to conceive that he should bring mankind into existence, unless he intended to make them finally happy." We can all be real people.

In our 250 years as a Church there has been a long list of <u>not</u> real people who have struggled with the right to be full human beings. When this building was erected in 1811 there was a pew in the back corner of the balcony, on my right, for People of Color. In 1882 an English Unitarian woman wrote about the issue of the suitability of women as ministers (Peart, 2008). "Women," she wrote, "are … actually much <u>deconsidered</u> by men. Would not their deconsideration be reflected on Religion itself it they were to become authorized ministers?" Just the fact that a woman promoted an idea could devalue that idea.

Poor people are easily considered as not real people. Could anyone in this country safely ignore the folks in New Orleans who lost homes and businesses in Katrina? Are they not real people? Or just not real enough to help?

When a group goes from this church to New Orleans to help build and rebuild they were affirming that the people there are real people. Working on Habitat for Humanity projects, supporting programs in Cambodia, Oxfam, The Unitarian Universalist Service Committee— anything that reaches across the divide between cultures, ethnicity, religions, ways of being is an affirmation of their reality. When we built the addition we included handicap accessibility—I know it was a legal requirement but it was also a moral requirement when we think of the people we made welcome. I have on my desk an invitation to attend a "celebration of love and commitment" between a friend and her female companion. Are they real people? Becoming a Welcoming Church is an affirmation of their being real. Being a Welcoming Church is a logical extension of the Universalism this church chose in 1828, a logical extension of the Unitarianism embraced here in the 1830s. We have developed as a non-creedal church and we have no religious test in order to belong. We are welcoming of people.

A E Housman in one of his poems from *A Shropshire Lad* (XXXII) (Housman, 1896) described our reason for being:

From far, from eve and morning
And yon twelve-winded sky,
The stuff of life to knit me
Blew hither: here am I.

Now—for a breath I tarry
Nor yet disperse apart—
Take my hand quick and tell me,
What have you in your heart.

Speak now, and I will answer:
How shall I help you, say;
Ere to the wind's twelve quarters
I take my endless way.

We have for 250 years walked hand-in-hand sharing what is in our hearts, helping one another, reaching out. May we so do for another 250 years.

June 2008

To Outgrow The Past

Our reading last Sunday was from William Laurence Sullivan, (Papers, 1982) "Coronation".

"To outgrow the past but not to extinguish it; to be progressive but not raw; to be free but not mad; to be critical but not sterile; to be expectant but not deluded; to be scientific but not to live on formulas that cut us off from life; to hear amidst clamor the pure, deep tones of the spirit; to seek the wisdom that liberates and a loyalty that consecrates; to turn both prosperity and adversity into servants of character; to master circumstances by the power of principle and to conquer death by the splendor of loving trust©©this is to attain peace; this is to pass from drear servitude to divine adoption; this is to invest the lowliest life with magnificence and to prepare it for coronation."

William Laurence Sullivan is mostly forgotten now. A few of us have copies of his autobiography and a book of prayers and meditations in our libraries. Sullivan died in 1935, so he probably belongs to a different generation; but something of his life is worth remembering for he was a person who outgrew the past.

Sullivan was born in East Braintree, November 15, 1872, his parents having emigrated from County Cork, Ireland, the previous year. After a public school education he was educated at Boston College and then St. John's Seminary for the priesthood, and was admitted to the Missionary Society of St. Paul, the Paulist Fathers, in 1899. Over the next 10 years as a Catholic priest he preached, served a church in Washington, D.C., taught theology at St. Thomas college in that city, had a number of articles about religion published, and became identified with the so-called "Modernists" in the Catholic Church. In 1907 Pope Pius X issued an encyclical calling for unquestioning loyalty to church dogma, and Sullivan, after two years of struggle with conscience and those in authority, resigned first his pulpit and then his priesthood. The next several years he wrote, taught, sometimes lived in poverty (at one point he was literally homeless, living on the streets of a city as so many homeless people do today). In 1911 he joined the Unitarian Church in Cleveland, was given status as a Unitarian minister the following year, and served a number of churches until his death in 1935, as well as lecturing, writing (including several books), denominational activities and mission work. Yes, we had Unitarian missionaries at one time. A group called the Laymen's League was devoted to growth and expansion and opened a number of new churches. A somewhat irrelevant but interesting fact is that during this same period there was a group in Great Britain that had a church in a bus complete with a small organ. They went around on Sundays parking in areas without Unitarian churches and inviting people in. I don't think it was very successful but it sounds a lot of fun.

In his autobiography (Sullivan, 1944) Sullivan wrote, "So at the end of a long journey I have come to this: the first article of my creed is that I am a moral personality under orders." Sullivan was never bitter and did not become anti-catholic. He remembered with gratitude and joy his training for the priesthood: "We were taught the practice of meditation; and the first half hour of every day was devoted to it. Besides, we made a daily visit to the chapel ... and in the evening we listened to spiritual reading for half an hour.... It will be seen from this that the Catholic church takes seriously the preparation of the soul of its aspirants to her clergy. Would that Protestant seminaries followed her example!"

In a summation of his source of strength, he says: "There is no species of training that I ever underwent to which I owe more than to the habit of regular periods of inner solitude. Solitary we must be in life's great hours of moral decision; solitary in pain and sorrow; solitary in old age and in our going forth at death. Fortunate the one who has learned what to do in solitude, who can see what companionship may by discovered in it, what fortitude, what content. By a great blessing I had an aptitude for these hours of quiet reflection and grew to love them, and with increasing use I loved them ever more deeply. To be alone and still and thoughtful bestowed upon me the richest joy I knew; and for this priceless cultivation I shall be thankful always."

Sullivan recognized a reality that for many of us is hard to learn: that we can outgrow our past, although we cannot extinguish it. Our past is with us all of our lives. We may try to extinguish it. We can try to forget it. We can pretend that it is not there. But if we try any of those approaches, we drag the past along with us as a burden unless until we come to that time when we, like Sullivan, can use what is good, and forgive what is not, live in the present, and move to the future. The word "jot" as in "jot and tittle" is derived from "yod" the smallest letter in the Hebrew alphabet; it sort of looks like a comma. A tittle is the dot above the letter "i" or a similar mark. When Jesus tells people that "one jot or one tittle" will not pass from the law, he is telling them that truth cannot be changed. It is not truth or reality that changes but our awareness and our interpretation of it that changes. The training that Sullivan received from his years of experience in the Catholic church and from his childhood could not be changed. What Sullivan did was to "reframe" them--that is, to find in them a different meaning. He could have decided, for instance, that all the years he spent learning

Catholic doctrine, learning to be a priest, being a priest, were wasted time and have been angry and bitter. He could have looked upon those years as lost. Or he could, as he did, look upon them as years of preparation and growth, practice and training, self-development and opportunity. And that is what he did. He even considered his time of homelessness as a time of learning and maintained an active interest in and support of those in poverty for the rest of his life.

All of us carry the past with us--all that we have lost and all that we have gained; all the pain and all the joy. Sometimes we need help in sorting out the losses and the pain. Victims of abuse (there are claims that as many as 1 out of 3 women are victims of some kind of sexual abuse before they reach adulthood; the number for men is lower but still significant) very often need help in sorting out their feelings. It is not that we can simply do some mental gymnastics and say that it doesn't matter. But it can be turned into something that has past; it is there, but it is there in the past. Not to be forgotten. Not to be repeated (abuse is very often a family pattern). Not to be used to judge ourselves as somehow "bad" and deserving of the pain. Not to be between us and our living, but to be what was while we move through what is toward what we hope will be. Evil experiences (or just plain bad ones) can be a basis for building empathy, compassion, and the skill to help others with pain in their lives. And that is a reframe.

It is after all, our past which makes us what we are today. Much of current social thinking seems to be irreligious; that is, without sense of purpose or moral framework. Life becomes "Just one damn thing after another" without connectedness or meaning or direction. The goal of life becomes to fulfill personal ambitions (as fed to us by the perception of "main-stream" thinking). The past becomes something not to be learned from but to be manipulated to serve our ambitions. We need to remember people like Sullivan who could describe himself as a moral personality under orders and in our best moments, strive for the same vision and the same hope.

October 1988

God as Mother, Mother as God

I think Motherhood isn't what it used to be.

Some historians credit Miss Anna M. Jarvis (1864-1948) of Philadelphia with making Mother's Day what it is. Her mother died May 9, 1904. Over the next few years, she organized memorial services for her mother. In 1907 the service grew to be large enough for her whole church. In 1908 the memorial was observed by the entire city of Philadelphia. In 1913 the day gained status as an observed day in the Commonwealth of Pennsylvania, and in that same year the U.S. Congress made the second Sunday in May a national observance beginning in 1914.

Prior to Anna Jarvis, Rev. Theodore Cuyler, a Presbyterian minister, would preach in the mid-1800's "God made mothers before he made ministers. There is a ministry that is older and deeper and more potent than ours, it is the ministry that presides over the crib and impresses the first gospel influence on the infant soul."

Flowers and praises and pictures of mother as the ideal sentimental being have been common, but that has changed with the feminist movement, women's liberation, and with more women working full time. Back in 1975 Martha Weinman Lear (Lear, 1975) could finally write about the bitter sweet aspects of Mother's Day. "What I remember vividly is that in my late adolescence," she wrote, "my mother bought a fine big white stove. It was her pride, replacing a despised cast iron model, and she cleaned it carefully after each meal. My grandmother, whose sight by then had gone quite bad, would drop food on the stove and leave greasy finger marks, and I can remember my mother cleaning up after her, scrubbing and rubbing and muttering angrily to herself."

Years later, Ms. Lear tells us, her mother comes to visit: "She tries to help in the kitchen.... And her sight is not good, and sometimes she takes dirty dishes out of the dishwasher and stacks them up on the shelves, and she leaves charred bits of food on my fine copper colored stove, and I find myself standing there scrubbing and rubbing, muttering angrily."

"Our mothers grow old," she concludes, "and we watch them becoming us, and ourselves becoming them, and whom do we extricate from what? And how? And do we pass this dear, murderous entanglement on to our daughters with the family silver? Often I wonder if this is not some ultimate form of liberation: the most painful, and the most elusive."

I think we are in the midst of a painful liberation, but a liberation none the less. Someone once wrote words to the effect that the great sin of the Hebrew slaves in Egypt (you have to dig out you memories of the Bible stories of Moses and the Exodus to appreciate this) was not that they were slaves but that they learned to accept their slavery. We grow comfortable in the way we live, and even define the world by ourselves. But every now and again someone jerks our chain and we have to wonder if our self-definition of the world is as normal as we thought it to be. Carol P. Christ in her book *Diving Deep and Surfacing* (Christ, 1980) tells us (from a feminist point of view) that "women's quest is for wholeness."

And in spite of the fact that a lot of people are not convinced that language does not make a difference there are a lot of people who contend that it does. Alma Graham, writing in 1974 (Graham, 1974) said: "If you have a group half of whose members are A's and half of whose members are B's and if you call the group C, the A's and the B's may be equal members of Group C. But if you call the group A, there is no way that B's can be equal to A's within it. The A's will always be the rule and the B's will always be the exception, the subgroup, the subspecies, and the outsiders."

We might notice for instance, that the Rev. Mr. Cuyler quoted earlier on the precedence of motherhood over ministry did not volunteer to change professions. Or we might notice our own habit of speaking of ourselves as Americans and having to explain with qualifiers about Latin Americans, Spanish Americans, Japanese Americans, Black Americans, etc. We used to talk about doctors and "lady doctors." We still differentiate between education for children and "adult education." As Maria Harris, a religious educator and writer tells us (Harris, 1995), "whoever owns a word owns a great deal more." Our language is not only how we communicate, "it is also an expression of shared assumptions."

Brother Lawrence of the Resurrection, monk, pot scrubber and mystic, writing back in the 1600's shifted his image of God in these words: "My most useful method of spiritual attainment is this: simple attention, and such a general passionate regard for God, to whom I find myself often attached with greater sweetness and delight than that of an infant at its mother's breast; so that, if I dare use that expression, I should choose to call this state the bosom of God, for the inexpressible sweetness which I taste and experience there." Or Mechtild of

Magdeburg (Herbermann, 1913) who wrote in the 1200's "God is not only fatherly. God is also mother, who lifts her loved child from the ground to her knee. The Trinity is like a mother's cloak wherein the child finds a home and lays its head on the maternal breast." Or Julian of Norwich (Jantzen, 1988) who left us with words such as "...God almighty is our loving Father, and God all wisdom is our loving Mother...." and "...though our earthly mother may suffer her child to perish, our heavenly Mother Jesus may never suffer us who are his children to perish." Jesus used such imagery: "how often would I have gathered thy children together, even as a hen gathered her chickens under her wings...." (Matt 23:37)

Their visions speak perhaps more truly than we have given them credit for. Their vision is of God as a wholeness containing not only the characteristics thought of as male but also the characteristics thought of as female; not only strength and power, but also gentleness and compassion, just as we discover in whole people, men and women, strength and power as well as gentleness and compassion.

It is wholeness that we seek. Not just women, and not just for women, but for all of us. Thus it is that we need to look at our images of motherhood and God and our use of words.

I don't think that a person can be fully a mother so long as they are trapped in some kind of idealization. Idealizations deny us wholeness because they deny us our humanity and our personhood. The perfect mother, the "divine mother" is an idealization, and it makes of the person something less than human. By idealizing women, and their role in society, for instance, we also have denied them access to an equal place in the world. The early experiments in co-ed education in this country in the latter part of the last century were, for instance, considered failures by many educators not because women could not be educated but because they excelled in such areas as math and science, and deliberate programs of steering women away from such subjects were adopted by many colleges and universities. How, after all, can we accept someone in crinoline and frills being the top chemist in the university? Or take such a person seriously? As fashion designers recently attempted to revive the mini-skirt, they learned that while it was great for recreational wear, most women with jobs and professions knew they could not wear one to the office, in the factory, in the laboratory, or in surgery and be taken seriously. By idealizing people we control them, or attempt to. By idealizing someone we deny them completeness as a person. The idealized mother is denied human frailty and weakness, is denied talents and strengths that do not fit the ideal, is made less rather than more.

Our concepts of God, on the other hand, can be as limiting. We do not want God (even if we don't believe in God) to be weak and vulnerable, less than almighty. A God who cannot be the source of the feminine in us as well as the masculine is only half a god at best. A view of nature that does not include the feminine as well as the masculine elements is only half a view of nature.

It is not the destruction of images that we look for; it is not the lowering of the status of women and mothers and God that we seek. It is their wholeness and completeness. So we celebrate motherhood, not as an idealization but because none of us are whole, none of us are completely human. God is not real unless that half of life is present in us and for us.

CLOSING WORDS

I took a deep breath and listened to
the old brag of my heart.
I am, I am, I am.
...Sylvia Plath (Plath, 1967)

May our hearts brag that we are. And may we be as whole as we can be. And may we help others be as whole as they can be.

AMEN

May 1988

Maundy Thursday

Down through the years there has been a great deal of debate over the exact nature of the communion service with some folks holding that it is symbolic and others maintaining that it involves an actual changing of bread and wine into the body and blood of Christ. There is a wonderful description of Martin Luther meeting with John Calvin and others in an attempt to come to some understanding within the newly formed Protestant churches of the 1500's; and Luther writing with his finger on the conference table "this is my body;" and every time someone even suggested that it was not quite that literal, his jumping up and pounding on the table and pointing to the words and yelling "is, is, is, is."

We are not that literal, and in fact, we will universalize the symbolism. For us, in this particular act and event and memory, lie our understanding of the sacrifices made by countless people, women, men, children, brave and weak, strong and foolish, wise and scared; even the sacrifices made by all living things that we might have the opportunity to live a decent life. Bread and wine are not only the symbols of the blood and flesh of people. They are also the blood and flesh of the earth which sustains us. They are the substance of the universe in which we live and move and have our being, the substance that gives us life and keeps us alive. The astronomers will even tell us that much of what is necessary for us to live, the heavier elements of iron and calcium, potassium and phosphorus, essential to us, are created in dying stars and then swept up in stars being born. It is the sacrifice which makes us possible. It is through our sacrifices that give new life and new hope to the world. And so it is from time without measure to time without end.

Real sacrifice is an act of love and an act of living. It is the giving of something of value for the sake of something of greater value. Real sacrifice is the giving of that which we prize for the sake of someone else. But more than that it also means living in such a way that other people benefit. This does not always mean putting aside all thought of self. It does not mean always giving others what they think they want. Sometimes the best help we can give to others is by our example and our courage and our strength and our taking care of ourselves.

Sacrifice is not something we do out of weakness or passive compliance to the wishes of others. Sacrifice is what we give out of our store of strength and conviction: our time, our energy, our goods, and our effort; not to serve ourselves only but to serve others and to share with others. Sacrifice is to acknowledge that other people are part of our lives, and that we are part of theirs; that we live not to ourselves alone but in a great web of being.

So we focus on a particular event in a particular time and place and use it to symbolize all of the sacrifices, all of the acts of giving, all the acts for the love of others, all the giving and receiving which make our lives not only possible but rich in joy and love, all the caring and love which make us able to endure pain and loss, and all that we give and all that we receive.

We are bound together in the bundle of life as we share in the substance of the good earth. Let us share in the symbol as we share in the reality.

THE MEAL. This is the broken bread, the traditional symbol of hospitality, the symbol of sharing, the symbol of sacrifice, the symbol of community in the bread of life. Take and eat in remembrance and peace. This is the juice of the vine, the token of self-forgetting, the symbol of sacrifice, the reminder of our share and common life with things upon this earth. Take and drink in remembrance and love.

BENEDICTION

Let us go forth in peace. May the blessings of truth be upon us. May the power of love direct and sustain us. May the strength of community sustain us from this day and forever. We ask in the name of all the prophets, and all the simple people, whose gifts of love made our lives possible and worth living.

AMEN

March, 1988

Not the Dream but the Reality of Life

We will be holding the annual meeting of the First Religious Society this afternoon at 4 p.m. followed by a potluck supper. The question could be asked, "Why do we bother?" Why do we keep a church and do all the work and pay out all the money. We end up with covenants and mission statements and goals and purposes. Sometimes it is useful to put all of that aside and ask ourselves, as members of what one writer terms the Sea of Faith, what is it that we seek?

The Rev. Forrest Church, senior minister of All Souls Church, Unitarian Universalist, in New York City in a new book titled *Lifecraft* (Church, 2000) tells us that the poet, W. H. Auden, while living in New York City, visited a bar and, sitting in a corner, studied the crowd. "He read traces of boredom, futility, and disillusionment. Turning over the placemat on his table, he penned this poem:

Faces along the bar
Cling to their average day:
The lights must never go out.
The music must always play....
Lest we should see where we are,
Lost in a haunted wood,
Children afraid of the night
Who have never been happy or good.

James Martineau, an English Unitarian minister who flourished in the middle 1800's (Hall, 1951), wrote that "Silence is in truth the attribute of God, and those who seek God from that side invariably learn that meditation is not the dream but the reality of life; not its illusion but its truth; not its weakness but its strength."

But we are Auden's people, wanting the lights on and the music playing constantly lest we be left alone in darkness and silence. I think that we get the sense that frenetic activity is a sign that we are doing something important. Incessant noise is an indicator of meaning. We live in a world with the technology to provide us with a lot of reasons not to be silent. Television, radio, telecommunication, CD's – I think now that you can show movies in the back seat of new cars so that your passengers won't be bored by your company or the scenery.

In the Sea of Faith there is room for silence and silence is where we find – if we seek.

Lao Tzu once said "One who knows does not speak: one who speaks does not know." So if I knew what I was talking about at this point I would say no more. But since we are all seeking always and we are great head-trippers, I will say more.

Psalm 46:10 tells us "Be still and know that I am God."

In the First Book of Kings, Chapter 19, Verse 10 following, the prophet Elijah has gone to Horeb, the mount of God. "For the Lord was passing by: a great and strong wind came rending mountains and shattering rocks before him, but the Lord was not in the wind; and after the wind there was an earthquake, but the Lord was not in the earthquake; and after the earthquake fire, but the Lord was not in the fire; and after the fire a low murmuring sound. When Elijah heard it, he muffled his face in his cloak and went out and stood at the entrance of the cave." And, the text tells us, spoke with God. "A low murmuring sound" is the New English Bible translation. King James and Revised Standard Version translation are the more familiar "Still small voice." In the New Revised Standard translation the passage is rendered "a sound of sheer silence." I like that, "a sound of sheer silence." Isn't there a 60's-ish song about the Sounds of Silence? Elijah when he heard it – or didn't hear it – knew immediately what it was and covered his head. In our culture we would have expected that the show of force would have shown where the glory and power was, but not so – in the silence is where it appeared.

Jesus said, "Consider the lilies of the field." In those lilies we are to find a message, but it will be a message spoken in silence.

The absence of God, the silence of God, is always troubling. We want answers. And we want answers now.

R. S. Thomas, Anglican priest, Welsh poet, (Davis W. V., 2007) in a poem titled "The Possession":

He is a religious man.
How often I have heard him say,
looking around him with his worried eyes
at the emptiness: There must be something.

It is the same at night, when,
rising from his fused prayers,
he faces the illuminated city
above him: All that brightness he thinks.

And nobody there! I am nothing
religious. All that I have is a piece
of the universal mind that reflects
infinite darkness between points of light.

Or his poem "Via Negativa":

Why no! I never thought other than
That God is that great absence
In our lives, the empty silence
Within, the place where we go
Seeking, not in hope to
Arrive or find. He keeps the interstices
In our knowledge, the darkness
Between stars. His are the echoes
We follow, the footprints he has just,
Left. We put our hands in
His side hoping to find
It warm. We look at people
And places as though he had looked
At them, too; but miss the reflection.

Among Buddhists the void at the center of the universe is spoken of.

William Isaacs in a book titled *Dialogue and the Art of Thinking Together* (Isaacs, 1999) points out that we are a very visual society – dominated by sight. Thousands of images are flashed "across our minds" by TV and Internet. Especially if we have cable or a satellite dish and like to surf. Click, click, click, click…. Isaacs says that we are bombarded with images and that while light travels at 186,000 miles per second, sound only travels at 1,088 feet per second. We get used to the pace and impatient with other paces. We have to practice listening. Isaacs gives six steps on listening:

1. Recognize how you are listening. Be conscious and be aware.

2. Notice what you are thinking. Note the difference between stored reactions and fresh responses.

3. Listen with more humility. Sort assumptions from reality.

4. Listen for sources of difficulty whether in you or in others. Don't just listen for what confirms your point of view; catch up with how others experience the world.

5. Listen for gaps between what you say and what you do.

6. Be still. By quieting the inner chatter of our minds, we open up to a way of being present that cuts through everything. Think of this as calming the surface of the waters of our experiences so we can see below to the depths and receive the meanings that well up from within us. These creative pulses may move in us, but often we are too busy to pay attention. Stand still and you will feel and know them."

William Lawrence Sullivan was a Unitarian minister, born in 1872, to a Catholic family. He was educated by the Jesuits and trained for the priesthood at Boston College. He taught theology and served as a parish priest until he resigned his priesthood in 1909 over questions of church policy and dogma. In 1912 he was admitted to the Unitarian ministry and served in that capacity until his death in 1935.

In his autobiography *Under Orders* (Sullivan, 1944) Sullivan wrote: "There is no species of training that I ever underwent to which I owe more than to the habit of regular periods of inner solitude. Solitary we must be in life's great hours of moral decision; solitary in pain and sorrow; solitary in old age and in our going forth at death. Fortunate the person who has learned what to do in solitude and themselves to see what companionship they may discover in it, what fortitude, what content. By a great blessing I had an aptitude for these hours of quiet reflection and grew to love them, and with increasing use I loved them ever more deeply. To be alone and still and thoughtful bestowed upon me the richest joy I knew; and for this priceless cultivation I shall be thankful always."

Gandhi was a fan of silence. He observed one day a week in silence – traditionally Monday during which he would not talk or listen.

The British imposed a Salt Tax on India during the Raj, and Gandhi complained that it was an immoral and unjust tax on the poor. The manufacture, distribution, and sale of salt were controlled through the tax mechanism. Gandhi wrote a letter to the Viceroy in 1930 pointing out that while the Viceroys salary was $233 a day the average Indian made 4 cents a day. This salary was paid out of taxes on salt, drink and medical drugs. The Viceroy refused to reply more than a "your letter has been received and noted" communication. Gandhi sat in meditation for a long time and when his followers asked him what they should do he replied that he had not yet "heard."

After several weeks Gandhi began walking, in silence, toward the ocean, 240 miles in 24 days. Thousands of people joined him along the route. When Gandhi reached the water he bathed in it then scooped up a some sun-dried salt on the shore – mining his own salt in contravention of the Salt Tax laws, triggering off violent and often bloody British countermeasures and beginning the period of non-violent disobedience which helped drive the British out of India. Rabindranath Tagore, the Indian poet and Nobel Prize winner (Roy, 1977), could then write that India was free and the Europeans had lost their moral prestige.

"The power of the way," the Tao Te Ching tells us;

The power of the Way will come into you
When you are empty like a valley or canyon
And therefore receptive to it.
You will then be sensitive to good and bad equally as they concern you
And will be able to test everything for its worth.

May, 2000

Lent

Lent is not much observed these days; it is more of a vague mention than anything. Lent is the 40 odd days between Ash Wednesday and Easter Sunday. Actually the traditional Lent observance is a fast, and encompasses 40 days, Sundays being excepted. The early tradition was to abstain from eating flesh and "all things that come from flesh" which means meat, milk, eggs, butter, and cheese products. In more modern usage the strictures against eggs and cheese tended to fade away and Lenten meals could be heavily loaded with fish, egg and cheese dishes. "What we forego by fasting is to be given as alms to the poor," according to Pope Saint Leo I (died 461 CE). A more modern treatment of Lent has been to give up something that we like – for instance candy and gum for children -- I worked once with a woman who would give up seeing her boyfriend for Lent. Fasting is still observed in some religious bodies. We recently observed the rather odd behavior, widely reported in the news, of various church authorities giving, or not giving, people permission to eat corned beef on St. Patrick's Day. There were even people driving from one diocese to another to be free of restrictions on eating meat that day.

Penance and a time of spiritual preparation are ancient religious activities. Islam has the observance of the fast of Ramadan that lasts a month. Judaism has Yom Kippur, the Day of Atonement.

The purpose of this type of activity is to mortify the flesh, as they used to say, or to remind us of "those things we ought to have done and have not done, and those things we ought not to have done and have done." An opportunity to evaluate and re-evaluate, repent, look over our lives and see how we are living. Not always a popular idea. Fasting can become mere form, having people decide that it is a big inconvenience to skip the annual corned beef and cabbage dinner causes us to wonder how seriously we might be taking the concept of Lent and fasting.

I think also fasting as a spiritual exercise doesn't mean a lot to us. Fasting isn't a very noticeable activity when a large percentage of us are on diets of one kind or another, sporadically or continually – many of us should be fasting for the sake of our health to say nothing of our souls. Fasting doesn't carry the same meaning when we have people with eating problems of various types, anorexia, bulimia, and over-eating. There are people who don't need any more excuses to abuse their bodies and souls by religiously sanctioned starvation. Fasting means something when we are short of food – and reminds us of how close to genuine hunger we might be. It seems almost silly to give up steak for lobster or give up spaghetti with meatballs for macaroni and cheese. Pointless when grazing on snack food can be our principle source of nutrition. I suppose someone eating potato chips all day has more need and less motivation to fast than someone who hasn't a supermarket to go to for food.

We become removed from the real world – the way we can in the world of computers – I cherish my personal computer, thanks to church people who have supplied me with recycled equipment and low cost up-grades over the years (and kept a lot of electronic paraphernalia out of the transfer station and trash system), and I value having a computer in the minister's study here at the church. I find e-mail great and have done some exploration of the web and all that. But a computer is for me really a fancy typewriter or adding machine – not the necessity it has become for many jobs and many people. But you know and I know that to go into a basic personal computer from the get-go costs $1,000 or more, and that it may cost $30 a month for a broadband connection. Driving somewhere recently I was thinking about computers – my son told me that he was planning to buy a new one and wanted to know if I might want to buy his old one with lots of extras and added memory and faster than the one I had and I was mulling over his offer and I was listening to the BBC on WBUR. They were interviewing a woman who works in a shirt factory (making shirts for Sears) in some Asian country where there were street demonstrations and civil unrest. She was saying that when the mobs and the army were facing off in the streets she did not dare go to work and so could not collect her pay of $1 a day which was the principal cash income of her family. "Yeah," I thought, "and she's likely to buy a PC real soon," and I was thinking of spending more than she makes in a year so I could have a "faster" computer.

We have to admire Pope John Paul II, Cardinal Law, and other Roman Catholic officials for their recent confessions of the sins of the church over the past centuries – sins of commission and omission involving other religious groups and individuals and their role in conflicts. Heavily criticized by many for not going far enough or not mentioning enough or being apologetic enough, but none of that was their intention – what the Pope was doing was confessing calling for repentance before God. The Pope spoke of the church using violence in the service of the truth and sinning "against the dignity of women and the unity of the human race" and not always being on the side of the poor and oppressed. Not always, as it were, being concerned about those forgotten people who earn a dollar a day. As incomplete or inadequate as some think the confession was it is certainly a beginning.

Discussing this with someone we know who comes from a long line of Unitarians and who is herself active in a Unitarian church, we began to speculate about just what it might be that we would confess to, what we would expect the President of the Unitarian Universalist Association to confess to in our name. "Arrogance" was the word we finally came up with. Arrogance as defined by our sense of superiority. Fortunately for us and unfortunately for the world, we are not the only ones afflicted with arrogance. The difference between us and the world around us is us, is it not? That if we claim to be, as our covenant says, people who love, people who seek truth, people who are devoted to service, how then can we claim to be superior to others?

The Pope was pointing out that the Body of Christ, which the Catholic Church claims to be, was injured by the sins against dignity and unity, the sins of rejection and exclusion. All of these sins, arrogance, rejection, exclusion, racism, sexism, contempt for cultures and religions; all of these and many more sins, are sins of separation. We could speak of them as boundary issues.

Edwin Markham (Shields, 1955) wrote a poem:

He drew a circle that shut me out
Heretic, rebel, a thing to flout.
But love and I had to wit to win,
We drew a circle that took him in.

Arrogance, our self-attributed superiority, is a way of shutting people out, shutting ourselves off from other people. Working on a prayer for forgiveness for Unitarians and Universalists I have gotten as far as sentences about learning the peace of understanding others, accepting the wisdom of knowing that we do not know everything.

Maybe Lent isn't really the time repenting our sins; maybe it is a time for breaking down boundaries.

The Rev. John H. Nichols (Nichols, 2000) of the Unitarian Universalist Society in Wellesley Hills comments on the story of Creation in the Jewish scriptures: Adam and Eve eat the forbidden fruit and lose their paradisiacal innocence. Not "Original Sin", which is not a Jewish concept, but innocence. They realize that they are ambitious, can be self-serving, deceptive, and all those things we all struggle with at least now and then. They also learn that "we are given a life of incredible freedoms and beauty." Nichols says, "In order to enjoy those freedoms we have to discover our boundaries." This means discovering our own personal limitation, our intervals between doing and reflecting, and those limitations to our behavior which we call kindness, courtesy and ethics. Nichols also said "The temptation is to push those boundaries. We may try to work longer, harder. We may cheat a relationship here for a short-term gain elsewhere in the hope that when each ball comes down we will be able to catch it. In the end it won't work. It never does. It never has."

Or, as Van Ogden Vogt (Vogt, 1951), a Unitarian minister of previous decades wrote, "It is mastery of form that makes us free."

We have discussed two sets of boundaries, those boundaries which separate us and are a cause of sin, and those boundaries which are recognition of the limitations on us as mortal humans in need of being part of a community to be whole and healthy.

Perhaps instead of thinking of Lent, if we think of it at all, as a time to repent sin we might think of it as a time to celebrate Spring and the newness of life by renewing out lives through the shifting of boundaries, taking the boundaries away which we draw around other people to separate them from us, and installing some of those boundaries around our own behavior. Discover and acknowledge – put a boundary around -- our own limitations instead of focusing on the limitations of others. Put a boundary around our own behavior in the interest of kindness, courtesy and ethical behavior instead of being judgmental of others. Set ourselves free of living in a constricted world while we have an over extended ego.

What would we be like if we took Lent, or some other occasion, to imagine what our lives would be like if we were free of the boundaries that keep us from knowing and celebrating other people and lives, and if we were constrained to give up those behaviors which prevent other people from knowing and appreciating us? Free to embrace life and be embraced by life.

April 2000

Living the Spiritual Life: Letting Go

One of my favorite Calvin & Hobbes (Watterson, 1995) strips goes: "Hobbes", the tiger, says "I love Fall. I like the cool days, the smell of leaves, the low sunlight... And the sky looks even more blue when the trees are yellow and red." "I dunno...," responds the little boy, Calvin, "I think Autumn is melancholy. Summer is over, and in a week or two everything will be hunkered down for the long, bleak winter. Nothing lasts," he says, "Fall is just the last fling before things get worse." "If good things lasted forever," says Hobbes scratching his head, "If good things lasted forever, would we appreciate how precious they are?" Calvin stands there watching a leaf flutter to the ground. "I like," speaks Calvin, "to have everything so good, I can take it all for granted." Hobbes replies, "I think the brisk air makes apple pie taste better too! Mm-mm!"

This cartoon strip is a paraphrase of a Rabbinic story: A child is walking with a Rabbi when they chance upon the body of a lovely song bird. "Rabbi," asks the child, "why did God make it so that beautiful things die?" "My child," responds the Rabbi, "We would not value what we had forever."

Perhaps it is the best theory of Theodicy. Theodicy is the study of why, if God is good, do death, disease, sin, disasters, and suffering trouble this world and the lives that inhabit it? Perhaps it is a lesson in valuing life and the good things of life; though, that hardly seems adequate as an explanation to those who suffer.

Part of the issue of learning to let go is learning to accept the spiritual advice that the way to happiness is to will the inevitable: "None the less, not my will but thine be done."

The painting behind our pulpit is a good metaphor for letting go: It could not possibly represent all the symbols of human beliefs, the human condition, and all the ways of believing. It does contain a broad selection, and is a work of religious art in that it represents our letting go of exclusivity and parochialism and embracing Universalism. It is a sermon, a theological essay in itself. Since we cannot discuss every issue of letting go, I am going to focus on one.

The pink triangle is included not because it is a religious symbol as such but because it represents the diversity in the human condition by reminding us that Gays and Lesbians are also part of the human family -- indeed, very often part of our family -- your family and my family, your friends and my friends, even you and me. We hear a good deal from some groups about homosexuality and how homosexuals should be excluded from the American community. President Clinton has promised to support legislation protecting -- not special rights for gays, but the civil rights of gays.

I believe that our sexuality may be broadly categorized under three headings: Normal sex, perverted sex, and perverse sex. Normal sex is basically what we will publicly acknowledge. Perverted sex is anything I don't do or don't want to admit I do, or which I accuse people of when I want to control someone's life. Perverse sex is anything which injures another, body, mind, soul, spirit. What is ordinarily called perverted sex is none of our business. Perverse sex is far more common and we like to pretend that it is not. We focus on perverted sex in order to keep attention away from perverse sex. The people who use positions of power, authority, trust, to impose upon the young, the weak, the vulnerable pretend that it is all right so long as the sex acts are "normal". We know a woman whose father began having sex with her when she was 12 and claimed that he was teaching her about sex so it was OK. On the other hand, the state of Maine had a referendum on a piece of legislation called "An Act to Limit Protected Classes" which is an act aimed at denying civil rights to homosexuals while the criminals who practice perverse sex are not included.

One of the reasons for trying to pass such a law is that it is a way of establishing an Us/Them separation, of forcing people to conform to our standards or normalcy. The law basically says there are those of us who are normal and you better be one of us or else. This is another way to say "all animals are equal but some are more equal than others" as George Orwell penned in *Animal Farm*. It would make lists of those people to whom the constitution applies, and, by leaving people off, those to whom it does not apply. Germany, under the Nazis, never really passed laws denying legal rights to people, they passed laws defining who were human and who were sub-human (who were us and who were "other"). Legal protection was denied to "others," the sub-humans, as defined by Nazi theorists. It is all a way of hanging on to our own little closed world.

Letting go means going on a pilgrimage of faith.

St. Anthony (250-355 C.E.), Christian Ascetic and desert dweller, pioneering desert father, taught his followers to consider Satan, i.e. evil, to be the most intimate of enemies and our own self. Satan tempts us from within through our own thoughts, impulses, desires and imagination. *The Gospel of Philip*, discovered in the Nag Hammadi library teaches us that hidden within each of us is the "root of evil."

"So long as we remain unaware of 'the root of evil within us,' *Philip* says, 'it is powerful; but when it is recognized, it is destroyed.'" "As for us," *Philip* continues, "let each dig down to the root of evil within us, and pull out the root from the heart. It will be plucked out if we recognize it; it takes root in our hearts and produces its fruits in our hearts. It masters us, and makes us its slaves. It takes us captive, so that we do what we do not want, and what we do want to do, we do not (cf. Rom. 7:14-15). It grows powerful because we do not recognize it.

Learning to let go requires us to confront the root of evil within ourselves: our own pride, our own hatred, our own fear, our own greed, our own desire to control the lives of others, our own projection of the roots of evil within ourselves upon other people.

Learning to let go requires of us that we follow the Biblical injunction: "Enter by the narrow gate. The gate that leads to life is small and the road is narrow, and those who find it few". (*Matthew 7:13-14*). What does that mean? It means going on a faith pilgrimage to discover what is to be found, rather than demanding that everything fit our preconceived notions. Too much of faith is depicted as walled in and constricted. Some Christian groups, for instance, has narrow definitions of who is a Christian and broad definitions of who is not -- who is not only not Christian but not even a good American or deserving of a decent life. We deny the freedom that is offered us; we especially deny that freedom to other people... We are blinded and stifled when we are more interested in restrictions and controls, especially those placed on others, than we are in discovery and awareness. As we go through the narrow gate we give up absolute answers for the journey of faith: faith in God, faith in the creative power of life and living, faith in our own ability to meet and embrace who we are becoming.

Learning to let go is often the result of growing and maturing -- our experiences as parents, pain and suffering, learning to love and building love, coming close to other people, experiencing pain and loss. Both pain and love teach us to be open to what other people offer us. Dorothee Sölle, (Sölle, Death by Bread Alone: Texts and Reflections on Religious Experience, 1978) a German Theologian, has written: "The more we love, the more people in whom we take an interest, the more closely we are bound to them, the more likely it is that we get into difficulties and experience pain." Or, as Hobbes put it, "If good things lasted forever, would we appreciate how precious they are?"

During the Middle Ages books were written with such titles as "The Craft To Know Well How to Die." Subtitled, "Know well how to die for you shall not learn to live unless you learn to die." Dying is letting go. We hold on to nothing in the end. We cannot take it with us; we leave it all behind. "Life," wrote Richard Boerstler, the Buddhist scholar in *Letting Go* (Boerstler, 1982), "Life means giving and taking; exchange; transformation. It is breathing in and breathing out. It is not taking possession of anything, but a taking part in everything that comes in touch with us. It is neither a state of possession or of being possessed. We are transformed by what we accept. We transform what we have accepted by assimilating it. We are transformed by the act of giving, and we contribute to the transformation of others by what we are giving."

Our religious quest, I believe, includes this transformation -- accepting and giving, being transformed and transforming -- becoming more humane and offering to others humaneness. Letting go is one of the religious acts which makes this possible.

October, 1994

Bound in the Bundle of Life

First a very short story, *The Old Man and His Sons*, from Ambrose Bierce (Bierce, 1899).

An old man, afflicted with a family of contentious Sons, brought in a bundle of sticks and asked the young men to break it. After repeated efforts they confessed that it could not be done. "Behold," said the Old Man, "the advantage of unity; as long as these sticks are in alliance they are invincible, but observe how feeble they are individually."

Pulling a single stick from the bundle, he broke it easily upon the head of the eldest Son, and this he repeated until all had been served.

Second a very short history lesson, *First They Came for the Jews*, by Pastor Martin Niemöller (Marcuse, 2000)

First they came for the Jews
and I did not speak out because I was not a Jew.

Then they came for the Communists
and I did not speak out because I was not a Communist.

Then they came for the trade unionists
and I did not speak out because I was not a trade unionist.

Then they came for me and there was no one left to speak out for me.

Bound in the Bundle of life (I Sam 25:29)

Carson McCullers, American writer, lived from 1917 to 1967. In one of her stories, set in the South, *A Member of the Wedding* (McCullers, 1946), (later made into a movie) she tells about a 12 year old girl who has become enthralled with the courtship and upcoming wedding of her older sister. In one scene the girl is speaking to the family maid about how wonderful the wedding will be and how much fun it has been to choose flowers and the wedding dress and a trousseau and all the other preparations. And how much fun the wedding trip will be and how she is looking forward to it. The maid startles her by telling her that she can't go on the honeymoon, it is only for the young couple, a special and private time for them alone. The girl breaks into tears, protests, they have to take her, and she makes a heartfelt plea, "They are the we of me."

A wonderful phrase: "They are the we of me." I think that every "me" needs a "we." Without a "we" we are cut off from the fullness of life, lonely, subject to emotional problems. Not having a "we" is not the same as solitude. Solitude is a choice, different from loneliness.

Solitude can be a source of growth, refreshment, renewal. Think of parenting, and how precious a few moments of solitude were when the children were finally in bed for the night, and the dog is asleep, and the cat has gone down cellar, and you and your spouse had quiet time. Loneliness diminishes us, makes us wish for something to fill the quiet.

There are many "we" choices for us: family, work, occupation, avocation, political party, social groups, many, many, more. All overlapping, intertwining. Churches are, in my mind, a "we" of "me," a place where we find a place to be. Every "we" is together for its own reasons. Trudi and I belong to a bridge group, we have our birth families and our extended families, and our own family. But churches, at their best, have their own reasons for being a "we."

As a child I learned an old Christian hymn, "Blest Be the Tie that binds." This was included in our 1937 Hymnal (AUUA, 1937), the old red one, but disappeared when the last two hymnals were published:

Our fears, our hopes, our aims are one,
Our comforts and our cares.
We share our mutual woes,
Our mutual burdens bear;
And oft for each other flows
The sympathizing tear.

What I like about our church, the Unitarian Universalist churches, and, truth to tell, some others, is that people ask questions. Many churches have answers that people have to fit into and accept. But most people have questions and as the UU Bumper Sticker from some years back says "To question is the answer."

When we ask questions we are freed from rigid thinking, freed from insisting that we all walk the same path. We give ourselves permission to be tied by love, respect, not sameness. As Hosea Ballou said, "We don't have to think alike to love alike."

Politicians, when they appeal to the worst in us, want us divided and separated; in other words, to make us weak and scared.

We must not be naïve enough to pretend that just because we have good will and want to work together that it will work. There are plenty of people who want us divided. There are many of us are selfish and want advantage with no care for others. But then hanging together with one another becomes more important. We need to transcend our differences of life style, age, politics, religion, etc. Granted, it is a struggle sometimes, or all the time. As Dr. Phil often asks "Do you want to be right or be happy?" Too often we only want to be right.

Tragedy can bind us together. This is the fourth anniversary of 9/11 and we are reminded of how tightly bound together we were as we responded to the death and destruction of that terrible event. How disappointing it is that our response as a nation to Hurricane Katrina and its destruction has been so confused and delayed. We have to ask ourselves, are these people part of the 'we of me' for us as a nation? Accusations are being made about neglect because of race and poverty, 'we are not poor so they are not us' thinking. I suppose we can put the best face on it and hope that the situation is the result of incompetency or stupidity, but the reality is that a city is ruined and up to a million people are homeless and countless thousands are dead and the people responsible for ordering action are now engaged in photo-ops and blaming other people for the decisions and non-decisions. But the final questions is, Are they 'we' or are they 'them'?

The events of the past few weeks point up what, in my mind, it means to be religious, to be a person of faith which is something I struggle with, not something I claim to be good at.

When I was a young mouthy twit I attended a summer Bible School run by a local Mennonite Church. The person in charge was an out-of-towner, a Mennonite Bishop from another state, who went around doing educational programs.

Anyhow I was extremely skeptical about the Biblical stories and one day I got into a conversation with the Bishop and asked him how he could "prove" the truth of the Christian story. We talked a bit and then he said words to the effect: "I can't prove the stories about Jesus and the things in the Bible. But I read the stories and think about the lessons he taught and I ask myself 'Is there a better way than this to live my life?' I make the choice to be a follower of Jesus."

I think we get easily bogged down in minutia of religiosity; just like the people in Gulliver's Travels who are fighting a war over whether, when spooning the insides out of a soft-boiled egg for breakfast, you should break the egg open at the big end or the little end.

We can have wonderful arguments about such things – people make their living doing just that.

But in the end, it is what we do and not what we say that matters, i.e. "by their fruits you shall know them." By our treatment of one another, our treatment of others, we show our faith.

September, 2001

Christmas Eve

"Be not afraid," the angel said to the shepherds. "You will find a babe wrapped in swaddling clothes and lying in a manger." "And suddenly there was with the angel a multitude of the heavenly host praising God and saying, 'Glory to God in the highest, and on earth peace among people with whom God is pleased.'" (Luke 2:14)

"Peace, goodwill among people." "Peace and goodwill." "Peace, goodwill toward people." "Good will to all people." "Peace to everyone." This is the message, it just depends on the translation you use.

We often think of peace as the absence of war, the absence of conflict, but that is a small and negative definition of peace. Jesus was born in a time of peace, the *Pax Romana* – three hundred years of Roman rule over Europe, North Africa, and the Middle East reaching from Ireland and the Southern border of Scotland to the borders of India. This era began with the consolidation of Rome's conquests by Julius Caesar prior to his assassination in 44 BCE. Roman rule could be tyrannical, people were exploited, slavery was practiced, repression of dissent was swift and brutal, but the rule of law and administration of justice were the ordinary experience of people. It was easier and safer to travel from the British Isles to modern Iran than it is now. Art, business, education, book publishing (slaves copied the books), flourished, and there were no major wars.

Peace is not just the absence of war. Peace is the presence of the things which make for the goodness of life: Public safety, a system to ensure justice, reasonable prosperity.

Peace is described by the Jewish prophet Micah (4:4) as "everyone shall live under their vine and under their fig tree; and none shall make them afraid."

Peace in the Bible includes the stranger being respected, and being able to walk safely down any street anywhere.

Jesus is called the Prince of Peace, picking up a term used by the Prophet Isaiah in Jewish scripture. Jesus lived a life of peace. Not peace in the passive sense such that he didn't get into trouble; he did get into trouble and was executed for his ideas. But peace in the active sense: forgive one another; love yourself and your neighbors and your friends and especially your enemies; help the stranger; don't be judgmental.

Be careful what you love, because it can take over your life. Live fully today and let go of the past and don't worry about the future. Do good, bless, pray. Don't be nostalgic for some imagined future of a foolproof life but know that the Kingdom of God is within you and within us. It is within our reach. We make it reality (or not) by how we live and what we do.

Feed the hungry, bind up the wounded, heal the sick, release the captives, visit the prisoners, make your presence a blessing to the lives of children, clothe the naked, and invite the street people to the banquet. Be honest, be faithful, be kind, and be truthful. Be little children and take innocent joy in life. "Go, and sin no more."

Forgive, and forgive, and forgive.

If we seek only ourselves we bring ourselves to ruin, if we give our lives to others we receive the gift of knowing who we are. "If you love me," Jesus told his disciples, "you will feed my sheep." What we let go of we have forever; what we hold tightly we lose.

All of this is so simple to say, so difficult to do.

We gather this Christmas Eve to celebrate peace in the birth of a child, the love of family and friends, the wonder and beauty of life even in the darkness of the year. May the blessings of peace be ours to give and ours to receive this Holy season and always.

December 24, 2000

Who is Jesus

One of the really funny television programs is the British sitcom, The Vicar of Dilby, usually shown on a PBS station. "British Comedy" is how they advertise the program. The Vicar is a woman struggling to keep a small, poor, rural parish going. The Vicar is gentle and respectful and funny. The other night they ran a Christmas program and the Vicar is teaching the children about the Christmas Story. "What is unusual about Jesus?" she asks, and one little child answers, with a big smile, "His name is a swear word."

In 1906 Albert Schweitzer – one of the geniuses of the human race – published his book *The Quest of the Historical Jesus* (Schweitzer, The Quest of the Historical Jesus, 1910). Schweitzer lived from 1875 to1965. He was active his entire adult life as an organist, an organ builder, a philosopher, theologian, historian, physician, author, one time principal of a college, one of those people who makes your mind reel when you realize what you could have done if you had done like him.

In order to write *The Quest,* Schweitzer started by going to his university library and gathering all of the books he could find about Jesus. He took them to his room to read. One imagines he made many trips, and sorted them into piles according to their approach, theological, philosophical, rationalist, and pious, and then plowed through each pile. All this while working as a principal of a college, writing books about Bach, organ building, organ playing, and beginning his studies at medical school.

When I was at Theological School one of my fellow students described Jesus as "a nice guy social worker." I don't know if he made that up or if he got it from somewhere else. Sometimes we would have conversations around the contrast between the religion of Jesus and the religion about Jesus. In Christian history classes we learned of the various theories and theologies of and about Jesus; that he was not the born Son of God but the adopted Son of God; that he was totally human; that he was human and God; that he was a spirit and had only the illusion of solid substance (this for people who believed that anything physical had to be corrupt); that he was never crucified but had someone take his place; that he didn't die but recovered and lived out his life in India; as well as the more orthodox Christian beliefs about the divine birth and the nature of the Trinity.

Back in the early part of the 1900s someone decided to interpret the story of Jesus, at the age of 12, stopping in the Temple at Jerusalem to discuss scripture and theology with the priests. His frightened parents found him and scolded him for not telling them where he was going and he replied – King James Translation of the scriptures: "I must be about my father's business." So the writer said God was His father, and business must mean business, so Jesus was saying that God wanted him involved in business in the sense of capitalism which proves that Jesus was a capitalist.

Books have been written contending that Jesus used hallucinogenic drugs, that he was married and had children (perhaps ancestor of some of the royal families of Europe), and so on and so on. General Christian teaching is that he was crucified, died, and on the third day rose from the dead. There is evidence that this was not a universally held view among early Christians. At least part of the early Christian community was a reform movement in Judaism considering Jesus a prophet rather than a divine being. One of the standard arguments in support of this is that the Synoptic Gospels – Matthew, Mark, and Luke – have parallel versions of the story with small variations except the birth stories and the events following the crucifixion. The theory is that the Synoptics, Matthew, Mark, and Luke, share common sources, perhaps their authors had access to a book now lost, called by scholars the Q document, and that each added material. The major differences in the birth and resurrection narratives lead to the argument that these portions of the story were added on by different groups of Christians and not part of the original story. There was a Jerusalem Christian group that appears to have been led by James, the brother of Jesus, which was dispersed when that city was destroyed in 70 CE by the Romans during the Jewish Revolt. The Jerusalem Christians, from what little evidence we have left of them, apparently did not teach a resurrection.

The concept of Jesus as Messiah comes from the Jewish belief that God would send a King, a Savior, a prophet, a leader, and that in spite of all the historical difficulties of the Jewish people, God would not abandon them. As historian Morton Scott Enslin (Enslin, Christian Beginnings, 1938) wrote "…in the perplexing book of life, the last chapter, and a singularly glorious one, was yet to be written." The differentiation between Jews and Christians came about over the issue of whether the Messiah had arrived yet. The people who became the first Christians were Jews who believed that the Messiah had come.

People often differentiate between the religion of Jesus as compared to the religion about Jesus. Jesus was a Jew, born, raised, lived, and taught in the Jewish tradition. He died as a Jew. His teachings are about how we should be faithful more than how the faithful will win and become top dog. He was strong on forgiveness and reform – "go and sin no more." He was an advocate for the poor and the oppressed which is very much in the Jewish tradition. Perhaps he was a political radical because it appears from some of the texts that he had have hung around with some radicals. And of course it is all subject to interpretation. There is the incident where Jesus is asked (Matthew 22:17 ff) if Jews should pay tribute to Caesar. Jesus asks for a coin and points out that the name and image on the coin is Caesar's. "Give to Caesar the things that are Caesar's," he says, "and to God the things that are God's." It seems an innocent enough answer but there is an argument that maintains that it was very radical. In Jewish thought the Jewish nation and people belonged to God so this could be interpreted as a revolutionary political statement. This is the difficulty we run into: how to understand the meaning of words brought to us over the gap of centuries and from ancient languages.

The religion about Jesus is what we most commonly think of as Christianity with its doctrines and dogmas and statements of faith. I don't think that any of us are going to come to a final answer that will satisfy everyone.

Thomas Jefferson, President Jefferson, wrote "I am a Christian, in the only sense in which he wanted anyone to be: sincerely attached to his doctrines, in preference to all others; ascribing to himself every human excellence; and believing he never claimed any other." Gandhi thought of Jesus as "...one of the greatest teachers humanity has ever had." Morton Scott Enslin (Enslin, The Prophet from Nazareth, 1961), a New Testament scholar summed up over 40 years of study by these words: "The one whom we call Lord, who stands for us the compelling expression of the longings and dreams of mankind, by the quality of his life, by his unflinching bravery and devotion, by his fidelity to his task, transformed his followers, not by miracles..., but by the life which he lived...transformed them into (...people) like himself, who recognized him for what he was, and thus saw God in him."

Schweitzer argued that Jesus "has been made the receptacle into which every theologian pours their own ideas." (Schweitzer, The Quest of the Historical Jesus, 1910)

I think that it is often fruitless to debate the nature of Jesus, person, myth, God or some combination. As a Unitarian Universalist minister I would observe that the most damage done by religion is over the issue of religion about Jesus. We are a species that prefers to have things neatly bundled. We want to know what people think, and we want them to think what we think. At certain points in history at certain places, having the incorrect thoughts about Jesus was considered a capital crime. However, seemingly there have always been "thought" police about some topic or another.

What we believe about Jesus is surely closely related to what we believe about the universe. As someone said, "We see things not as they are, but as we are." Jefferson was a rationalist, a believer in an orderly and ordered universe. Gandhi was a believer in truth and believed that truth would prevail. Enslin was talking about the triumph of the human spirit, an idea popular in the years leading up to WW II.

Some of us believe in, think they know, a universe which has in it things other than the merely rational. For such people definitions of truth may have different dimensions. The one thing we may all share in common is not necessarily concepts about, but concepts of how to behave and relate to each other and the world which is essentially what is of most practical significance in the religion of Jesus.

There are endless numbers of biographies of Jesus. Some are good, some are interesting, and some are just terrible. Most are trying to fill Jesus with their own ideas.

Schweitzer concluded that we were unable to bring Jesus into our modern categories: "He will not cross or ford the river of time with us. Jesus of Nazareth will not suffer Himself to be modernized. As an historic figure He refuses to be detached from His own time. He has no answer for the question, 'Tell us Thy name in our speech and for our day!' But he does bless those who have wrestled with Him, so that, though they cannot take Him with them, yet, like those who have seen God face to face and received strength in their souls, they go on their way with renewed courage, ready to do battle with the world and its powers." (*Quest*. P. 312)

"He comes to us as One unknown," Schweitzer wrote to finish his book, "without a name, as of old, by the lake-side, He came to those who knew Him not. He speaks to us with the words: 'Follow thou me!' and sets us to the tasks which He has to fulfill for our time. He commands. And to those who obey Him, whether they be wise or simple, He will reveal Himself in the toils, the conflicts, the sufferings which they shall pass through in His Fellowship, and, as an ineffable mystery, they shall learn in their own experience Who He is." (*Quest,* P. 403)

December 3, 2000

Little Saint and the Smell of Flowers

The Roman Emperor Diocletian lived from 245 to 313 of the Common Era. He served as Emperor from 284-305. His great claim to fame was his decision to eliminate the Christian problem in the Empire. He ordered Christians found and destroyed. The ultimate test was the accused's willingness to make a sacrifice to the Pagan Gods. Pretty strict lines were drawn. The law was generally whatever the governing officials said it was, and the Christians suffering persecution generally did not welcome back anyone who had betrayed them. Sacrifice or be executed on the one hand, sacrifice and be considered an apostate by the Christian community on the other.

The orders from Rome were simple, find and destroy the Christians. On October 6, 303, the proconsul Dacien was holding court in Agen in the south of that part of the Roman Empire which is now France.

A girl was brought before him and he questioned her, who are you and why are you brought before me? She was 12, not yet 13, showing the first signs of puberty. She was of a noble family, her father a minor government official.

She stood straight and brave before the gathered crowd and the soldiers and the proconsul and replied: "My name is Foy, and I am a Christian." "Since I was a little child," she said, "and first learned of Him, I have loved the Lord Jesus Christ."

"Oh, my dear," said the proconsul, "Your mother and father await you now in the house of your birth. Think of the grief you would cause them. You, their beloved daughter, their firstborn."

"It is Him my soul loveth," she said.

"Come, come my child," said Dacien, "sacrifice to Diana as your parents would have you do."

Many of the Christians had been warned of this day and had fled or gone into hiding. I remember Sister Laetitia teaching a class in Spiritual Formation who told us that Christians should be willing to die for Jesus but not to commit suicide for Him. Foy was young and innocent and thought that she would be safe if she stayed home. As Philip Pullman says "Innocence is not wise and wisdom is never innocent." She was not wise. But she was faithful.

She made the sign of the cross and prayed for strength.

"No," she said. "No, I will not."

Quietly, gently, the proconsul spoke to her of her parents waiting for her at home, of how they had already begun planning for her wedding and had been seeking a suitable husband for her, how she would bear children and run a household and raise a family.

Foy replied that she wanted to love only her Lord, have Him as bridegroom, give her life to Him and if not Him nothing else was satisfactory.

"Come now, my child," said Dacien, "You speak so charmingly. I have no wish to torture a girl as tender as you. Come sacrifice to the goddess, sacrifice to Diana. You need only reach out with your fingers and touch a grain of the salt and the incense placed on the altar there before you. Do that. Just that. And I shall release you."

She did not move.

But she spoke: "Your gods and goddesses are but demons, they are evil spirits…. The product of men's imaginings….

"There is but one God. He who came down from heaven for us and himself man… who healed the sick … who suffered and died for us…. No, I will not sacrifice to Diana, nor will I touch your incense."

They stripped her and beat her with rods until she bled. She refused to sacrifice.

They placed her on a grill, a brass frame and lit a charcoal fire beneath her. Legend is that a sudden shower extinguished the coals, but she must have been badly burned.

By now there were people in the crowd shouting, "What evil has she done? What evil?"

So the officials ended it. They removed her from the grill and forced her to kneel and she was beheaded. The people in the crowd who had begun to cry out for her were attacked and bludgeoned to death.

During the night her body was taken by Christians and hidden under stones on a plateau near the city. Later, when people went back to bury her, the scent of roses came from her grave and, moving away the rocks, they found all of her wounds and burns healed, the only sign of her beheading a red line around her throat.

Her father, the legend tells us, was the one who turned her over to the prosecutors. He had done it, he said, to teach her responsibility.

How many times have those of us who are parents, spoken those words, "Be responsible"?

"It takes a village to raise a child," we are told. Foy, like all of us, as all children, was raised by several villages. Two are worth mentioning. The first was the village of Christians in her community, those people who had told her and taught her the Christian message. Who were they? They were perhaps servants, neighbors, family friends, relatives, or even other children. The second was the village of her family and community loyal to the state and the society of the day.

The children of today are raised by more than one village: the village of adults, the village of school, the village of peers, and the village of commercial exploitation. An article in the Boston Globe, "Underage of consent," (Globe-Staff, 2000) discusses sexual activity of children sixth grade and under, and the way that peer pressure and the entertainment industry help form and guide their actions and values. I think that the article would be painful reading for anyone with children in that age range.

Unitarian Universalist congregations around the country have embarked on a new program going under the acronym of OWL, standing for "Our Whole Lives." We are starting with 8th and 9th grade people. The program is designed around the themes of Self Worth, Sexual Health, Responsibility, Justice and Inclusivity. In its totality the program is designed for all ages with appropriate material at every level. This is an attempt by our "village" to teach our young decision making based on non-exploitive values. With the village concept in mind this is a program involving parents and adults rather than lecturing to children. If Diocletian had been a Unitarian Universalist or if Dacien had been or her father, they might have said to that 12-year-old girl "We respect you and want you to be safe and healthy." They surely would not be willing to sacrifice her for the sake of the State.

What graven images do we sacrifice to or kneel our children before? The news is not good is it? Tuberculosis and polio are again major diseases in our world because the developed nations have cut back on their medical aid to the developing nations; the 50 cents that it costs to vaccinate a child is invested instead in military supplies or is no longer available at all as the wealthy become less and less willing to support foreign aid. We sacrifice our own children to the profit which can be made from "X" rated or nearly "X" rated music and movies, violence and sex and rampant consumerism.

One of the appeals of Christianity in those early days was the message that we were not owned by the state and that we had worth and dignity and value as human beings.

The message today is still about worth and dignity and value.

I have a PS.

One of the consistent legends that applies to the early saints is that when their bodies decayed instead of the usual bad odor they would give of the scent of flowers, often roses. One of the legendary marks of saintliness in the early church was to be able to go without bathing, even for years on end, and exude a lovely, sweet odor.

We were in New Hampshire when I was reading the book about Saint Foy (Green, 2000). There were four of us sitting at a table and a fifth person in a corner of the room in an easy chair reading a great thick spy-thriller type book. At the table one of us was doing a crossword, another was reading, the third person was doing a jigsaw puzzle, and I was reading.

I had just read a passage about how Foy, though a saint, still delighted in childish things and liked to play practical jokes.

I had read that and was thinking about it when I noticed a distinct smell – flowers, perfume. "Do you smell that?" I asked no one in particular. The jigsaw puzzler said that she didn't smell anything and went back to her puzzle then looked up surprised, puzzled, and said "You mean that?" and then I smelled it again. The other two people at the table smelled it and then a fourth time though only three of us noticed it the last time. "It was like a woman wearing perfume kept walking through the room," said the jigsaw puzzler. I don't think that it was the perfume of roses, but I am unsure of that. The person in the corner noticed nothing. I went back to reading.

November, 2000

Time Like An Ever Flowing Stream

Life, we have often said here, is a process. Not an event, but an ongoing process of growth and change, development and differences. When we stop growing we start dying. Not all processes work the way we want them to or expect them to. I started working on this sermon and got two pages written and lost them to some kind of can't-open-that-document-thing with my computer. Which I suppose is a lesson in life, "Life is what happens while you make other plans." My other plans were great, but life happened and I lost two pages of text. Which event is probably more of a sermon than what I could have said or have to say. It reminds me, though, that not everything turns out the way we want it to or expect it to.

What I had intended to talk about is time, so I will talk about time. St. Augustine is cited as having said, "I know what time is until someone asks me to explain it." Time is the working out of the processes of the universe and involves our awareness of that process. Someone once said, "God invented time so that everything wouldn't happen at once."

In Western thought we tend to think of time in terms of the words of one of our hymns this morning – "an endless flowing stream." Other thought systems view time differently – more as a lake than as a stream in Eastern thought and among some groups time is thought of as cyclical – today is yesterday come again. Yesterday come again brings to my mind the images of sheets of paper and computer screens. I used to write all of my material on sheets of paper, never of course, using the same sheet of paper twice. I write on the computer now and I use the same screen over and over and over.

I was reading something about the "Big Bang" recently – that theoretical instant in which the universe of which we are a part came into being. An infinitesimal bit of disturbance exploded and expanded into the universe. What caught me was the statement that time and space spewed forth along with energy and what became matter. It bends my mind to think of time and space being created with matter and energy – but why not?

The process that supports our existence had a beginning and presumably can have an end – the Big Bang presumes a beginning and an end. Divine creation presumes a beginning and an end of time is prophesied. Some thought goes to an open-ended universe, open at both ends. If we believe in the Big Bang, the question is what was there from which the conditions for the Big Bang could occur. If we believe in Divine creation then the Divine existed before the act of creation…. And on and on. In mythology there is the great worm, or dragon, Ouroborus, depicted as holding its body in a circle so that it could nourish itself by feeding on its own tail – the symbol of time as an endless self-feeding, self-renewing process. Ouroborus is used on various symbols associated with the Unitarian Church in Transylvania, and I don't know the significance except for the symbolism of time. We are reminded of that old concept of "Out of nothing, everything."

The process of time is dealt with differently by different people. My paternal ancestors in Northern New York have a symbolism that always fascinates me. The Croghan, NY, Mennonite Church buries the dead in very neat rows in chronological order. Not family plots, no choices, no fancy tomb stones just name and dates. I think that it says something about being in the process, not being set apart or having a special status. The process goes on though the parts may change.

"Everyone" it has been said "is irreplaceable, but no one is indispensable." And we are reminded of that over and over by the process of life. I think this important for all of us to remember as we deal with this time of transition; personal transition for Trudi and me; institutional transition for this church and congregation. Transition involves us in endings and beginnings; beginnings and endings can trigger a sense of loss. It certainly does for me. "Enjoy the last times you will do things," I have been told, and so I do. The Christmas Eve service, at 5:30 this afternoon, was the 25th I have conducted here – never even managed to have the flu and forced to stay home. Christmas Eve services will continue, even if we are not together.

What will we do? This church will continue to serve its members and friends and this community as it has for over two centuries now. Trudi and I will ease into our future. Trudi wants to move to California where the warmer weather and the mountains draw her. My personal choice has been to return to Northern New York and raise chickens. Trudi reminds me that I would probably go nuts in about 3 weeks. I think that she is correct, but when we reassess our lives we, or at least I, think about the life I have not lived. The life I have not lived is the country life in which I was born with chickens in the backyard. The other very real possibility is part-time or interim work in churches, though I think that we will take some much needed rest and vacation time. This is something like a sabbatical for renewal and contemplation. Perhaps spend some serious time writing and collecting rejection slips for my poetry. I have a collection of biographies and novels about Jesus that I want to read through, and a pile of poetry books I want to spend a lot of time with. Trudi and I need to have more time for each other.

I would like to tell this congregation what it ought to do, could do, should do, but a very wise person said to me once that "It is not nice to should on people" so I will practice what I know I need to do and let go of the future. Except for one thing. I really hope that when you get your next settled minister, one of the things you will want her or him to be a part of is the student intern program at one of the area theological schools where Unitarian Universalist Ministers are being trained. These are Harvard or Andover Newton or Boston University. I really believe that this church has made a great contribution in helping with the training of ten people for the ministry. Our First Religious Society has a great reputation at Harvard Divinity School. This congregation has been excellent with students, and there are other churches right now grateful for your work and contribution. I hope this will be a permanent part of the life of this church. I also think that the students have made a great contribution to the life of this congregation. I know that it has been a real benefit for me to work with students.

Second exception: Continue to take care of this lovely old building.

Third exception: Take good care of each other.

We now move into a time of planning. With most transitions we don't always have time to plan but in this case we do, and this congregation is in the process of moving on to what it will become: An interim minister for a year or two years in order for planning and evaluation to take place, building a profile of this church and who they want for a minister. It is a process that is creative and community building. Creative in focusing on how to grow into the future (not to define growth as numbers only, but also in terms of program and spirituality and outreach), community building in that success depends on common effort. Eventually, in order to call a minister, this congregation will have to vote on a candidate. The nature of the position is such that a mere majority is not usually considered adequate (this church has by-laws that require more than that) and some ministers insist on as much as a 90% or higher vote. People have to work together, discuss together, share together, to achieve that type of agreement.

The day was a year at first
When children ran in the garden;
The day shrank down to a month
When the boys played ball.

The day was a week thereafter
When young men walked in the garden;
The day was itself a day
When love grew tall.

The day shrank down to an hour
When old men limped in the garden;
The day will last forever
When it is nothing at all.

The words of Theodore Spencer on the passage of time (Spencer, 1948). A little sorrowful perhaps but accurate – when we are young we think we are immortal, as we grow older we come to know how precious time is, and how precious is our time together.

January 2001

On Letting the Bears Rejoice

This is a sermon to honor the Buddha, in keeping with the flower arrangement which is in honor of the Buddha's birthday.

The 96th Psalm, verses 11-13, tell us:

Let the heavens rejoice and earth be glad,
let the sea and all within its thunder praise,
let the land and all it bears rejoice,
all trees of the wood shout for joy
at the presence of God
for God comes, God comes to rule the earth!

The first time I read that verse I misread it making the third line read "let the land and all its bears rejoice." I have decided that that is a more inspired reading than "all it bears rejoice" so I am going to leave it that way for this morning: "let the sea and all within its thunder praise, let the land and all its bears rejoice, all trees of the wood shout for joy, at the presence of God...."

I like the concept of rejoicing bears I think it wonderful to want the bears to sing and dance and rejoice, and all of the other wonderful beings that share this earth with us should rejoice with them, and so should we.

As the ecological crisis deepens around us and we become more and more aware of how fragile the life system of the world is we also become more and more aware of the need for better ways of resolving the issues and solving the problems. If we are to transport oil at the risk of the environment, for instance, is it possible to lower the risk, raise the ability to handle spills, and most of all, is the oil use important? One would hate to think that the environmental disaster in Alaska had at its roots frivolous uses of energy and petroleum products. I was in a super market the other day watching someone set up a display of disposable plastic containers for storing clothes. The display person noticed me and said I could buy one for $2.49, "No," I said, "I was just contemplating the creation of more plastic trash when we don't know what to do with what we have already." "Yeah," said the person, "I agree," and went on labeling the packages. Sea otters are dying by the hundreds so that we can have oil to make junk like that.

What we need are not more promises and technology, nor would it help us to abandon technology. Technology is not the issue. What we need is a change in us, so that the promises will be kept and the technology well and properly used. We need to turn from our greed and self-centeredness, arrogance and selfishness, and know that to heal the earth we have to heal our hearts first. We have to be open to new possibilities and widen our concerns to include the total global picture. We have to care about the bears as well as ourselves. "Our goal," writes Charles Cummings, a Cistercian monk, "is to forge a lifestyle that is sustainable within the limited resources of the earth. Affluent individuals and countries may have to accept a simplified lifestyle either voluntarily or reluctantly and by necessity" (Cummings, 1989).

We need to change our attitudes toward life and the world in which we live. We have become, in psychological jargon, dissociated from the natural order of things. Our Western tradition has built up a concept of division between us and the world, us and parts of ourselves. We divide ourselves from each other by use of class and category (race, religion, age, gender), we divide ourselves from our self by not recognizing our own wholeness to include our physical being as well as our mental being. We divide our religion from the natural order of the wholeness of things by denying our own bodies and the reality of our sexuality. We fragment ourselves by not recognizing that completeness is in relationship. We divide ourselves from wholeness when we assume that we are a different order of life than the living beings around us. We divide ourselves from wholeness when we assume that social or political or economic theories are the meaning of life rather than life being its own meaning. We divide ourselves from wholeness when we assume that the Biblical charge to have dominion over the earth means absolute power to misuse or use, abuse or dispose, of the earth and all it contains as we please. The replay of the Creationist controversy in education is part of this. The attitude on the part of some people that we are a special creation and this concept should be taught in the public schools is a skirmish in the ongoing ecological battle. Are we part of nature or superior to it? The concept that we are superior to nature has consequences that we already don't like. I would argue that the Jewish and Christian traditions out of which we come are not inherently corrupted by this division. The division is social and cultural. On the other hand, the division is so much a part of our way of thinking that sometimes it helps to look through the eyes of another faith's tradition.

Buddhism has been gentler with the world than the Western traditions have although not always. Japan which has a strong Buddhist tradition is heading for its own ecological disasters and has been slow to realize that extinct is forever when it comes to cranes and other life forms. But Japan and modern Asia are playing the Western game of development at all costs and need to take another look as we do at what they are doing. In fact we all suffer from overdoing the modern cult of economic development as the meaning of life.

Buddhism is perhaps more holistic than Western traditions have been. Buddhism does not separate life forms in theory the way Western thought can and often does. "Buddhism," writes Gary Snyder, "holds that the universe and all creatures in it are intrinsically in a state of complete wisdom, love and compassion, acting in natural response and mutual interdependence. The personal realization from the beginning state cannot be had for and by oneself, because it is not fully realized unless one has given the self up and away" (Snyder, 1988). From a Buddhist perspective he goes on, "The 'free world' has become economically dependent on a fantastic system of stimulation of greed which cannot be fulfilled, sexual desire which cannot be satiated, and hatred which has no outlet except against oneself, the persons one is supposed to love, or the revolutionary aspirations of pitiful, poverty stricken marginal societies." And he begs us to consider the "joyous and voluntary poverty of Buddhism" accepting the world as one vast and interrelated network in which all objects and creatures are necessary and of worth.

Thich Nhat Hanh, a Vietnamese Buddhist tells us that "We have built a system which we cannot really control. This system imposes itself upon us, and we have become its slaves and victims. Most of us, in order to have a house to live in, a car to drive, a refrigerator, television, etc., must pledge our time and our lives in exchange. We are constantly under the threatening pressure of time. In former eras we could afford three hours for one cup of tea, enjoying the company of our friends in a serene and spiritual atmosphere. We could organize a party to celebrate the blossoming of one orchid in our garden. But we can no longer afford to do these things. As we say, time is money. We have created a society in which the rich become richer and the poor poorer, and in which man is so caught up in his own immediate problems that he cannot afford to be aware of what is going on with the rest of the human family" (Hanh, 1988).

Our future does not lie in the past so it is no good trying to undo the modern world.

Our future does not lie in the present, so it does no good to simply continue blundering along the way we are.

Our future lies in the future (an obvious tautology but an important one), and we need to think of the future.

In order to do that properly we need to seek wholeness and healing for ourselves and the world, seek to know the difference between what we need and what we want, be concerned for all people and all living things as we are concerned for ourselves and those around us.

April 9, 1989

Why Give Money to the FRS, and How Much

I will offer you the most exciting thing I have learned this past week: Why is a sheet of paper oblong? As in a book, typewriter paper, newspaper, and all of that? Answer at the end of the sermon.

First Timothy, in Christian scripture tells us that "The love of money is the root of all evil." This is commonly misquoted as "money is the root of all evil." We are ambiguous about money, which is perhaps why we are so reticent about it. But love of anything can be a root of evil. We speak of money, then, not as a source of evil and contention but as part of life and even a necessity of living.

First, I am going to talk about goals.

In order to do a proper job of setting goals we need to remember the acronym, SAMM. It stands for the four things which make goals workable: Specific, Achievable, Measurable, and Meaningful.

How do we set the goals:

Have each pledge unit, individual or family, set a pledge goal.

To find the pledge goal each unit -- individual or family -- would take a pencil and a piece of paper, write down annual income and take the following percentages.

For people with income below the median income in Carlisle of $83,985 a goal of 1%.

With people at or above median income to average income, which in Carlisle is $108,724, 1.5%

For people above $108,724 a goal of 2%.

I could bore you with statistics demonstrating that these are not unusual or unreasonable numbers. Latter-Day Saints (Mormons) give over 7% on the average. In traditional Jewish and Christian thoughts the requirement was a tithe or ten per cent. Catholics, Lutherans, Congregationalists, and Methodists give, on average, in this one to two percent range.

Now we shall evaluate these goals with SAMM.

The first test, Is it Specific? Yes.

The third step is M for measurable, but I am taking it out of order because I want to speak about the budget which is also measurable. A pledge is a specific number and the collector sends out quarterly notices to inform people how they are doing on their pledge.

Budgets are measurable.

Our budget for the current year 1996/97 is $163,000 of which the greatest part, close to $110,000, is for salaries.

Pledge and Plate Offering and Gift support from the congregation for the year 1996/97 is projected to be about $83,000. Activities (Fall Fair, Holiday Fair, Service Auction, odds and ends) bring in another $16,000. Rentals bring in $8,500. The shortfall, $54,500 (a third of our budget) is drawn from trust fund income. To continue using all of the Trust Fund Income for current expenses assumes that the FRS will never be faced with extraordinary expenses in the future and that the stock market will continue to grow at an accelerated rate indefinitely. To spend that income involves spending income from money left in trust to protect the long term stability of the institution for things such as renovations, improvements, development, and building up future resources. Now it is used to pay the current heat bill, buy postage stamps, pay repairs and salaries, subsidize the expense of running the church. FRS may be living beyond its means. To cut the entire $54,000 from the budget would require firing staff. Even to cut half the amount would require getting rid of at least one position. Someone has advanced the argument that some of the programs such as Youth, Religious Education (at least in part) is outreach and development and I agree with that. Some Trust Funds were given specifically for the care and maintenance of the building ("upkeep of the edifice" in the quaint language of the will) and it is proper to use them for that. There is nothing wrong with dipping into reserves now and them to tide us over a difficult time. It is not a good long range policy to continually use up all of the income from trust funds.

The second test, the one we skipped: Is it Achievable? Boston Magazine for April 1996 reports the median household income in Carlisle is $83, 985. The Boston Globe for February 6, 1997, reports the average household income in Carlisle is $108,724. On their chart of "Power Suburbs" Carlisle ranks second only to Weston as a "Power Suburb" in the Commonwealth of Massachusetts. The June 30, 1996 of Worth magazine ranked the communities in the United States by median income and value of houses, ranked Carlisle as the 184th wealthiest community in the United States on a list of the top 300. And the June 21, 1996 issue of the Carlisle Mosquito reported that 2% of the Carlisle population, or about 90 people, fell below the poverty line.

Achievability may be problematic for some. If a family is divided on their religious commitment, adjustments need to be made such as dividing their pledge between two institutions or giving the goal amount to one, or whatever works for that family. The goal may be problematic for financial reasons: tuition and school expenses for children, medical expenses, expense of caring for aging parents, preparation for aging and retirement, being down-sized or uncertainty about future financial condition, or extraordinary expenses of any kind. Just trying to live in this area may be an extraordinary expense: the cost of living in the Concord area is 145% of the national norm. Goals can always be adjusted downward or upward, perhaps the next step would inspire upward adjustments.

The big test is the second M. Meaningful.

Probably the most important issue is how meaningful supporting the First Religious Society is.

St. Paul, in his Second letter to the Corinthians, chapter 4, verse 7, wrote "But we have this treasure in earthen vessels...." We do not a claim to perfection. We are all human and can be short-tempered, inadequate, less than what we should be or want to be. We are earthen vessels -- all made of common clay. This church is an earthen vessel but in the earthen vessel of this community there are treasures.

The clay is the body, the treasures are the soul.

Thomas Moore, in his book *Care of the Soul* (Moore, 1994), wrote "It is impossible to describe precisely what the soul is. Definition is an intellectual enterprise anyway; the soul prefers to imagine. We know intuitively that soul has to do with genuineness and depth, as when we say music has soul or a remarkable person is soulful. When you look closely at the image of soulfulness, you see that it is tied to life in all of its particulars: good food, satisfying conversation, genuine friends, and experiences that stay in the memory and touch the heart. Soul is revealed in attachment, love, and community."

The soul of this church is revealed in our activities which include the following:

Worship Services, Music Program, Religious Education, Coffee Hour, Visiting Friends program, Social Concerns Committee, Ministerial Concerns Committee, Student Minister program, Weddings, Funerals, Memorial Services, Women Spirit, and a Men's Group. We support Oxfam, The Unitarian Universalist Service Committee, have supported and plan to take up again Heifer Project International, collect food and money for the Open Pantry of Greater Lowell, and other groups.

We house the Cambridge Society for Early Music "chamber music by candlelight" program, the Red Balloon, the Food Coop, Savoyard rehearsals, and other community activities.

This church community is with people in time of crisis, death, grief, sorrow, and in joy.

We encourage and support the spiritual journeys of people. Life is worth living, people are worth loving, each of us is unique yet in our uniqueness we create a pattern of love and hope and meaning. We respect diversity and find the sacred in the whole of creation.

We teach that the meaning of life is found in the spiritual and the material, the body and the soul.

Our body is the fabric of our physical being: our flesh and bones, circulation and breathing, digestive process, thinking, feeling. It is the vehicle of our existence in this world. The body of the First Religious Society, what we spend the money on, is building and heat and lights, maintenance and renovation, chairs and choir music, postage and newsletters, the Risograph and the Xerox and the paper for producing Orders of Worship, Staff salaries and District and Denominational dues, juice for the Church School and coffee for coffee hour, coffee pots and candles, our beautiful historic building standing in the center of Carlisle as it has stood since 1811 and we hope will stand gracing the lives of others in 2011 and 3011 and 4011.

What the meaning of the FRS is to any individual or family or group of individuals is not ours, or mine, to say. But as a human being has to attend to both body and soul to feel whole and holy, so this institution has to attend to both soul and body to be holy and whole. That takes the support of the living as well as the money of the generations turned to dust.

And now the answer to why a sheet of paper is oblong. It is because sheep are oblong. Paper, when introduced into Europe, was a substitute for parchment which is cured sheep skin. Books were made by folding and trimming a sheep skin, and the first book paper was made to mimic the size of sheep skins so that it could be folded and trimmed to the traditional sizes.

February, 1997

The Goodness of Life and Death

We say over and over, and it is worth saying over and over, that life is a process, not an event. And, as with any process, it is both finite and infinite -- that is, my individual life is a finite process with a beginning and an end, yet, my individual life is part of the whole process of life; it is part of the existence of the universe and arises from that existence. The process of which I am part is as vast and infinite as the Universe itself.

What does that mean; what value does it have; and what has it to do with Easter?

What it means and the value it has is that we are more limited by our definitions than we are by reality. We try to encompass the meaning of the infinite in a few words; we try to come up with neat little definitions of ultimate reality. There is a story of the Buddha, who, one day was questioned by a disciple: "Why is it," they asked, "that you don't tell us about God and other theological matters?" The Buddha responded, in so many words, "why do you trouble yourself with such questions when you don't know how to live with your neighbor?" "Learn how to live," he continued, "and the rest will take care of itself." "The religious life," according to the rather longer version in the Buddhist texts, "... does not depend on the dogma...." (Ballou, 1948). The religious life depends on how we live.

From the Christian tradition we have the passage in I John which tells us, "Let us live for one another, for living for another comes from God and corresponds to God's life. .... No person has ever seen God, but when we live for one another we participate in God's life...." (Sölle, Not Just Yes and Amen:, 1983)

I know that there are people who find that too ambiguous, and for them there are those who discuss dogma. For us there is the question of living.

Easter is about life and living.

Paul Tillich (Tillich, 1955), one of the more famous theologians of our century, wrote "The word 'resurrection' has for many people the connotation of dead bodies leaving their graves or other fanciful images. But resurrection means the victory of the New State of things, the New Being born out of the death of the Old. Resurrection is not an event that might happen in some remote future, but it is the power of the New Being to create life out of death, here and now, today and tomorrow. Where there is a New Being, there is resurrection, namely, the creation into eternity out of every moment of time. The old Being has the mark of disintegration and death. The New Being puts a new mark over the old one. Out of disintegration and death, something is born of eternal significance. That which is immersed in dissolution emerges in a New Creation. Resurrection happens now, or it does not happen at all. It happens in us and around us, in soul and history, in nature and universe."

Resurrection is religious living. Living for others. Letting go of living only for ourselves. The acceptance of life and death as part of the infinite process of which we are a part, in which we participate.

We get rather enthralled, at times, with the flowers and the birds and all of that Spring-time stuff, and rightfully so. The flowers are lovely. I have grown especially fond of crocuses over the past few years and keep putting more and more in our yard. Snowdrops make Spring a reality. But that is only part of what Easter is about. It is a physical manifestation of the renewal of life. Easter is also about the renewal of life in each of us: the living for others, the learning to make the lives of other people as full as we are able. That is the spiritual side of Easter. It is also where the reality of Easter is to be found because what we do for each other, what we do for others, is the physical manifestation of Easter just as surely as the crocuses are the physical manifestation of the coming of spring.

Resurrection comes from living for others, and therefore transcending time and place, living in eternity, as we live, in Dorothee Sölle's translation of the passage from I John, for each other and therefore live God's life.

March, 1991

An Incident In The Life Of Three Little Pigs And One Big Bad Wolf

The other day the-three-little-pigs, played by our 3 years and 3 months granddaughter Stefanie and the big bad wolf, played by me, had their standard encounter with the-three-little-pigs hiding in their brick house (which is disguised as the knee hole under the computer table). Having pulled the chair/door tightly shut and defiantly proclaimed "no, no, no, not by my chinny chin chin" the-three-little-pigs laughed as big-bad tried to huff and puff his way in. Having finished that scene, big-bad awaited developments. The chair pushed back and the-three-little-pigs invited big-bad in. So the bunch of us huddled under the table and the-three-little-pigs asked "Do you want lunch?' "What is there?' asked big-bad, wondering where the story was going. "Broccoli and lemonade" said the-three-little-pigs. Having finished lunch big-bad asked, "Well, what do we do now." The-three-little-pigs thought a bit and then whispered, "have a piece of quiet." And so we did, and we enjoyed it very much.

Most of us can use a piece of quiet now and then. Vacations used to be planned around big pieces of quiet. Folks would go to places, cottages and houses and isolated places. We knew one family who owned their own island off the coast of Maine, no phone, no electricity, no neighbors and they would go there in the summer for 2 months. Every few days to a week they would chug ashore in a motor boat to get supplies and pick up any mail or messages at the general store. The Rev. Thomas Starr King, Universalist and later Unitarian minister – he who was credited for saving California for the Union when the Civil War began by his speeches at rallies – when he was serving churches in Boston would take off for the summer and hike the White Mountains. King described Conway as being his vision of heaven (this was before development). Vacations now are being offered to us which are one unrelenting round of activity – If a piece of quiet is offered it is a very small piece. A piece of quiet is healthy. When we plan vacations we should plan to include quiet time, for ourselves and those with us, we really don't need to be entertained all the time.

William Henry Davies (Davies, 1911) wrote a poem in 1911:

What is this life if, full of care,
We have no time to stand and stare—
No time to stand beneath the boughs
And stare as long as sheep or cows.

I shouldn't classify it as great poetry but the sentiment is worth taking with us.

And, yes thank you, I will have another piece of quiet please.

May 1, 2000

Waiting For

The millennium is upon us. In a little more than a month we will be in the year 2000. This year is supposedly measured from the birth of Jesus, though there are no accurate records and the date is, at best, a guess. There has been some controversy over just when the next millennium begins with the math types pointing out that 2000 is actually the last of the series starting with 1001 and that the actual turn of the millennium will be when 2001 is ushered in. Ordinarily we don't start counting with Zero, no "Zero, one, two, etc.," until we reach nine, we start with one and count "one, two three, etc.," until we reach ten. There was no year Zero, in the counting system for the years upon which our Western Christian defined calendar is based the counting goes directly from "1 BC' to "1 AD." Zero was not used in the West when the calendar was devised. On the other hand, it is all arbitrary anyhow – a columnist in the Boston Globe recently pointing out that one of the First Nation Cultures of the Americas, Mayan (I believe it was), had a calendar with a 500 and something day year based on the orbit of Venus around the sun. Go figure.

What has really surprised me was learning that according to a treaty signed in 1880, The Meridian Treaty, the official time worldwide is Greenwich Mean Time. And that the year 2000 officially begins at the stroke of Midnight (measured now in little bits of a second) at Greenwich which is 7:00 pm here. Astronomers keep track of things by Greenwich Mean Time so that there is no ambiguity caused by local time zones. So officially 7:00 pm, December 31st is the end of this century and the beginning of the next. The suggestion of the columnist which I pass on to you is celebrate twice, once at 7:00 pm, and once at midnight, or, if you really want to go big time celebrate this year and next so you get in 4 happy new year times.

We mention all of this because a lot of people anticipate the Millennium as the coming of the Apocalypse, the end of the world when God and the Devil will finally duke it out with pestilence, disaster, famine, war, monsters and armies of angels from heaven and angels from hell sweeping across the face of the globe in a splendid and supernatural version of blitzkrieg. It promises to be a spectacular show. One hates the thought of missing it. The Israeli government is presently preparing to deal with outbreaks of violence by apocalyptic Christians convinced that if they start a war, God will intervene on their side.

Advent, in the Christian calendar, is a time of waiting and preparation. The beginning of Advent is determined by one of those conflations of dates that is just odd enough to make us accept it as sacred. Advent begins on the Sunday nearest the feast of St. Andrew which is on November 30. The variance of the calendar allows the first Sunday of Advent to fall on any date from November 27th to December 3rd. For commercial reasons some of us don't like a Christmas season that varies in length by a week from year to year. In fact the Christmas season gets pushed back to Thanksgiving and even Halloween. The original intention of Christians observing Advent was to have a time of preparation, a time to meditate on, and be aware of, the spiritual values and significance of the life of Jesus and their own lives in faith.

A time of anticipation and preparation, but a nice time; the anticipation of the Holiday, Christmas legends and customs, family gatherings, carols, and all that goes with the holiday. And the rest – the vision, the hope, the promise of Peace and Joy to all that share life. The realization of the truth of the words of the Doxology Marguerite Shaw has us sing together sometimes on Sundays – "From you I receive, To you I give, Together we share, And from this we live." That is part of the hope of the Christian interpretation of the life of Jesus. One of the great teachers of the early Christian church, Origen (185-254 CE), taught us that anyone who brought hope or salvation to another was a Christ in their life. This parallels the Buddhist teaching that any sentient being is capable of acting as a spiritual guide to another, and therefore, a Buddha to them. This realization is a part of Christmas, knowing that we can reach out and give hope to others, that there are people who can bring hope and love and peace into our lives. We can be Christ to one another; we can be Buddha to one another; we can bring peace, comfort, and hope to one another.

The presents are nice. I really enjoy Christmas presents, but that is not what Christmas is about. Christmas presents are a modern custom. Stephen Nissenbaum, in his 1996 book, *The Battle for Christmas* (Nissenbaum, 1997), points out that present giving was developed by the commercialization of Christmas. Santa Clause, for instance, was brought to life in this country in the 1820's with people quickly accepting the legend that they were carrying on an "authentic, ancient, and unchanging Dutch folk tradition." Nissenbaum points out that previous to the modern observances of Christmas, beginning in the 1800's, Christmas was observed as a time of heavy drinking and carousing. The wealthy in England, for instance, were expected to put on an open house for their servants and workers complete with the best food and drink available. Ongoing as part of this tradition, to this day, according to Nissenbaum, British military officers are expected to serve food to the enlisted men in the mess hall. "Wassail" which we sing about in some of our Christmas doings, is considered a benign custom where friends and neighbors roam about and sing to each other and end up drinking something hot at the finish. Originally it was observed strictly along class lines with the farm hands and laborers in the village going to the homes of the well-to-do for food and drink, and the well-to-do knowing that they had better produce if they wanted the goodwill of the workers during the coming year. Sometimes a "trick-or-treat" atmosphere prevailed, and it could be unpleasant. Our Puritan founders in New England, the people who founded this church among others, are depicted as pretty grim people in a lot of ways. They did not celebrate Christmas and at one time in Massachusetts such celebrations were illegal. It was not just a mean-spirited attitude on their part; however; it was the nature of Christmas revels and activities in Great Britain that they were rejecting.

We have commercialized Christmas, and now what some of us wait for are the statistics about the sales figures. We may await the coming of Santa Clause and the gifts. We may wait for many different things. Eric Berne in his book *The Games People Play* (Berne, 1964) published over 30 years ago claimed that "Waiting for Santa Clause" was a polite name for "Waiting for Death." According to Berne, waiting for Santa Clause is a substitute for waiting for the education, the job, the inheritance, the invention, the perfect mate, the inspiration, and is actually putting off living until death ends the waiting for the end.

Our Universalist forbears taught a doctrine in this church for a good part of the last century which called for waiting for the apakatastasis, a double-barreled Greek word for the restoration of all things to their original state of harmony and peace, i.e. a return to the Garden of Eden. It was an end event, not of destruction and terror, but an end of reconciliation, health, comfort and hope for all.

I wonder about the people who look forward to the end of the world – the apocalyptic vision as recorded in the Christian scriptures with the massive terror and destruction. It strikes me as an immature desire to get back at all those people who didn't appreciate me. It is the kind of fantasy we often have in our youth. Or perhaps it is like the video games where the point is to destroy the enemy in an orgy of blood. Except of course, if God does it, it must be all right to smash and burn and kill. "The final struggle" between Good and Evil, God and Devil will wipe away all the bad stuff. Maybe it is just laziness – if we fight the "War to end all wars" or the "War to make the world safe for Democracy" we can coast the rest of the way and not be responsible for continual effort. The Universalists had a different approach; they wanted all the bad stuff made whole again, so that we could all go on living and caring for one another.

One of the great religious insights is the importance of awaiting the present. "Take no thought of the morrow," said Jesus, "for the morrow shall take thought for the things of itself." "Be here now," is a Buddhist goal. Live in the present, it is the only place we have. But we keep waiting... for something.

I think the important thing here is not to come away thinking that we are waiting for the wrong things, but that we discover what it is we are waiting for. Or maybe we never discover what we are waiting for. Perhaps it is like "be here now,' no big deal but extremely important. Maybe we will discover that it is the journey and not the destination that is important. "The journey itself is home," according a Zen Buddhist master.

Recently we discussed the concept of Congregational Polity and recalled that the Salem, Massachusetts First Parish has a covenant going back to 1629 in which the members of the church do "bynd ourselves to walke together." This is a journey, to walk together and to walk gently.

Advent is a time of waiting, anticipation. A time of looking forward. We recall the words of James Thurber the writer and cartoonist (Thurber, 1996): "Let us not back in anger, nor forward in fear, but around in awareness."

But today, well lived, makes every yesterday
A dream of happiness
And every tomorrow a vision of hope.
Look well, therefore to this day.

November, 1999

Gratitude

The word "Gospel", as in the Gospels of Matthew, Mark, Luke, and John, means "Good News." The word is derived from the Old English *god spell*, meaning good tidings or good news. It is a translation of the Latin *evangel*, which also means good news. One of the bits of good news we are offered is illustrated in the story of Jesus and his disciples walking in a grain field. As the Gospel of Mark (2:23ff) tells the story: "One sabbath Jesus was going through the grain fields; and as they made their way the disciples began to pluck heads of grain. The Pharisees said to him, 'Look, why are they doing what is not lawful on the sabbath?' And he said to them, 'Have you never read what David did when he and his companions were hungry and in need of food? He entered the house of God, when Abiathar was high priest, and ate the bread of the Presence, which it is not lawful for any but the priests to eat, and he gave some to his companions.' Then Jesus said to them, 'The sabbath was made for humankind, and not humankind for the sabbath....'"

This good news is the suggestion that the rules are to help us and not to hinder us. Saint Augustine is quoted as having said "Love God, and do what you will." The assumption being that your motives are proper to begin with. Not freedom as a license to do anything we feel like doing, but freedom to act for the good of people. Good news always has bad news associated with it, and the bad news is that this approach asks us to be responsible and careful.

Albert Schweitzer, the famous jungle doctor, lived from 1875 to 1965. Christian theologian, organist, organ builder, philosopher, and writer, he decided to earn a medical degree at the age of 30 so that he could go to Africa to help people. Schweitzer developed as a moral standard the concept of "The Reverence for Life." But he also pointed out that to be reverent meant to set priorities: "It is wrong", he said, "to casually destroy living things". "Thus", he said, "there is a moral difference between walking along the road and knocking over flowers with a walking stick and cutting those same flowers if you are making hay. The first is casual and unnecessary destruction; the second is part of the process of harvesting a crop to produce food for animals and people". One of the stories of Schweitzer is that he had a pet pelican (Schweitzer, The Story of My Pelican, 1965); his hospital in Africa was next to a river and the pelican was found injured. Schweitzer nursed it to health and fed it and it walked around the house and sat on a perch but could no longer fly well enough to live in the wild. Eventually the bird got ill, and Schweitzer would stop and look at it every morning on his way to the hospital. He would grab the bird's beak force it open, throw in a penicillin tablet, and go to work. One day he looked at the bird, tossed in the tablet, and said to a visitor, "If this bird isn't better by tonight I will have to wring its neck." The visitor protested, remind him of his "Reverence for Life," scolded him for not being more generous to the bird. Schweitzer agreed with the visitor that "Reverence for Life" for his guiding principle and then said, "this bird is taking my time and attention and using penicillin pills. I have 50 patients at the hospital, some of them are critically ill and need all the care that we can give them. I have to choose between the people and the bird, and I choose the people." The story has a good outcome, by evening the bird was better – perhaps it understood that it was the last chance to recover.

Schweitzer was echoing the words of Jesus about the Sabbath being for the benefit of people.

Our gratitude, at least some of it, should be for the teachings and examples that let us know that the, as St. Paul said, "the letter kills, but the Spirit gives life." We have our churches and our religious communities; we have those people who by example and faith show us the way to live.

There are rules for how to act religious. Real faith is a matter of what is in our hearts and souls. The rules are useful. Faith is what gives life.

At this feast of Thanksgiving there are no rules for how to be grateful – gratitude comes from the heart. May we find in our hearts the well spring of gratitude and share that gratitude with one another.

November, 2000

The Crisis

We are, some days, close to overwhelmed with crisis. Libya may be making chemical weapons and our government may be on the verge of bombing the factory. In California a Health Maintenance Organization has canceled its contract with the state to take care of welfare patients because it costs $150,000 to deliver a baby whose mother is addicted to crack, and they are getting more and more such cases (an ordinary delivery costs $3,000). New York City, and possibly Massachusetts and other places, is being overwhelmed with the cost of taking care of people with AIDS. The forests of Brazil and everywhere else, including New Hampshire and Carlisle, are being cut down for development of the land, degrading the air we breathe, changing the climate, destroying all kinds of life forms. An earthquake has devastated parts of Armenia. The European Economic Community says that American raised meat is unfit for human consumption because of the use of the same type of hormones that athletes use with such disastrous results. Terrorism in the form of a bombing on an airplane is back. Arabs and Israelis continue to threaten each other. Air quality in New England continues to deteriorate. The government is talking 60 years and uncounted billions of dollars to clean up the radioactive wastes they deliberately dumped in places like Ohio because it was a good way to cut budget or save money. Thousands, millions of people in this country are homeless, and people are not being educated for the jobs of the future, and even with a job you often cannot afford a place to live. The highway system is crumbling and cities are faced with gridlock as more and more people try to jam their cars into them.

The folks in government keep telling us that they can solve all of this if we will raise their salaries, and do it without raising our taxes and then they do nothing significant until a crisis hits and then tear around trying to do something about it until it passes and then they wait for the next crisis to hit. Crisis management it is called isn't it?

The old doggerel: "When in trouble/ Or in doubt,/ Run in circles,/ Scream and shout."

It does us no good to be overwhelmed by all of this. It is tempting to throw up our hands, or simply to become bitter or angry or despairing. What we really need is a dose of steadiness. Most of these problems are long range and need long range solutions and long range planning. You and I cannot do that by ourselves, we can expect the politicians, the government, the people in charge, to do that, we can support and encourage the people and the groups who are working on long range solutions and long range planning. None of our problems have to be overwhelming; all of them took time to develop and will take time to alleviate.

Let me shift ground for a few minutes. My soul is corrupted with a streak of either violence or anger (or maybe it is because so much of my mind and spirit were formed during WWII) and certain types of military imagery have a deep and lasting appeal for me.

One of my favorite images is the French Foreign Legion. Cable TV came to our home this past summer and one of the first programs to pop up was an hour on the history and current status of the Legion. I loved it, watched every second, regret deeply that our VCR wasn't then hooked up so that I could have recorded it. I want to see it again. I feel guilty because I know better; there is no glory there only pain and suffering and people's lives destroyed. Though sometimes I try to rationalize it about maintaining public order and all that rot.

However, there is some good in all of this. It has been a busy year. There is a lot going on in church. I have been taking a course and music lessons. There are home and town activities, commitments to live up to, books and magazines to read, a flurry of weddings to conduct, UUMA meetings to attend, a ministerial support group to lead, cats to be fed, and the dog has to go out. Very much like the world in which we live, one crisis after another, though my crises are certainly minor compared to the bigger ones. But remember the French Foreign Legion story. One of the scenes repeated several times is that of the Legion marching. They sing as they march and one of the songs they sing is set to the tune of the Triumphal March from Aida, a slow march. The Legion, says the narrator, marches at 88 steps a minute. It always has, it always does, it always will. Far less than the 120 or that is standard for other armies. It is their pace, they practice it, and they use it.

Which brings us to spirituality. A lot of times we come around to spirituality by the back door. I had a teacher, Sr. Laetitia, who used to say that "God saves whom God chooses in whatever way God pleases, so who are we to question where wisdom comes from?"

One of the goals of spirituality is to help us achieve balance and rhythm in our lives. Take time for the really important things as well as the busyness of life. Watch the sunset, make love, pray, meditate, talk to each other, keep silence, savor food, listen, and "hold precious all that we cannot hold forever." Thus the Foreign Legion find your pace (Thoreau spoke of marching to a different drummer) find your pace and march to it. It is knowing who we are and what our natural pace is.

It is trusting our own instincts and being self-directed. It is seeking our place in the rhythm of the life of which we are a part.

Setting a pace forces us eventually to sort out what is important from what is not. Sometimes when trying to do everything, we set a frantic pace and thrash around busy, busy, busy; having no time for the recreation of the self; no time for recreation; having only the constant pressure of being more and more busy. I recently piled up a week's supply of mail and paper that I have not yet processed and there was six inches of it. What I did was discard most of it, delegate some of it, pay attention to a bit of it, recognize that I can't, in fact do not want, to treat all of it as worthy of my time and effort. And I don't feel guilty as I used to, because now I have that image of the marching Legionnaires, 88 steps a minute. Rain or shine, cold or hot, parade or battle, if you march, you march at 88 steps a minute. Gandhi did not talk on Mondays he maintained total silence as a spiritual discipline. Thich Nat Hahn took Thursdays off even during the days when the South Vietnamese government was trying to suppress the peace movement he was involved in. "Sir, they are raiding your office and taking your papers!" "It is Thursday, I will see to it tomorrow." It is a true story. Eighty-eight steps a minute regardless of what others expect or want or demand. Enough sense of internal assurance to know that the pace is right.

We give up a lot to be busy: exercise, time for we loved ones, contact with the earth (I found planting day lilies this past summer a spiritual renewal), playing music, reading for pleasure, writing for self-knowledge, prayer time, meditation to quiet the rush and listen.

A lot of what we need now is spiritual, not because religion has easy answers to the crises of the world, but because a mature faith can provide us with steadiness and sense of purpose. I was impressed, for instance, with the head of the Church of Scotland speaking at a funeral service in Lockerbie on how we need to avoid the senseless murder of innocent people that revenge and vengeance lead to. That is the kind of rock hard steadiness we need in this world and the kind of advice we need to hear more of and listen to more often. We get caught up in the heat of the moment and forget that we need to make decisions not only for today but for tomorrow, not only for ourselves but for our children.

Crisis will be with us a long time. We can flop from one to the other. We can bury our heads in our own corner of the world. We can get bigger and better weapons. We can try to pretend that nothing is happening until it comes knocking on the door. Or we can pick and choose those groups, those causes, those people, moving in the right direction and stay with them and support them and be ourselves steady and moving toward the future.

January, 1989

System or Special Creation

Reading: Exodus 20:22©25

Some of you are better at this than I am, but one of the concepts we have to understand if we are to understand how people and the world and the universe and everything else works is systems theory; which is to say, the recognition that everything is interconnected. Someone has suggested that the flutter of a butterfly wing in Kansas changes if only by an infinitesimal amount, the weather in Boston. The ecological problems we are having result from changes which have ramifications system wide. For instance the Japanese and the Americans get in conflict over the Japanese recognition of the interlocked system of economics, agriculture, culture, and politics. We want to sell them rice at prices far below what they can produce it for. They are aware that this will cause major changes in the whole order of their society driving farmers off the land (as we have) and creating either a new urban poor or the need for new jobs, shifting use of income, changing political loyalties, making the country more dependent on imported food, changing where people live, changing the use of the land; consequences we can only speculate on, but potentially, as we have had in this country, an avalanche of social change. Our government insists that it be done in the name of our economic system. The Japanese resist because they do not want to deal with the long term changes it will trigger. I suppose the theology of it is lost, at least to most of us, but we act as if we believe that we are a special creation.

In fact, one of the opening rounds in the current debate and concern over ecology was published as "The Historical Roots of Our Ecological Crisis" written by Lynn White Jr., and published in 1967 in "Science" magazine (White, 1967). The Christian church is blamed by White for setting the attitude that "We are not in our hearts part of the natural process. We are superior to nature, contemptuous of it, willing to use it for our slightest whim." As an ex-governor of California said, "when you've seen one redwood tree, you've seen them all."

It is too long to go into but the Christian church is both guilty and innocent of the charge. Christian thought, as part of Western thought and culture in general, has supported the idea of superiority, but, and it is a big but, the Christian church and Western culture are the inheritors and promoters of the Roman concept of domination and superiority. The Christian fault is not one of originating a bad idea but of not examining carefully the ideas of the culture of which it is part. People cutting and burning the Amazon jungle millions of acres a year see it as a crusade, taming the land and bringing civilization. They talk about "cleaning" the land when they remove the jungle. In "Hymns for the Celebration of Life," a UUA publication from 1964 (Foote II, 1964), is a work by John Holmes that goes "Peace is the mind's old wilderness cut down...." A parallel image civilization is order and control, not chaos and nature.

Scholars can and have documented the period of time at which the role of women began to shift from equality to subservience in the Christian church and it is closely related to the time when the Bishop of Rome and Roman cultural ideas began to co-opt the running of the church. There has been, and continues to be, in Western culture and religious institutions, a struggle between those who promote the masculine images of dominance and control and order and those who promote the feminine images of nurturing and caring and sharing. The male imagery is civilization and mind, the female imagery is culture and body. The struggle is actively engaged in today. The Roman Catholic church is heavily and rightfully criticized for not allowing women full expression of their abilities and talents. I heard a nun recently say that she had reached the point where she was wondering if she could remain in a church which did not allow her equal status. The Communist world is troubled by people who have had enough of central control and high flown social theory and want to assert their own culture and run their own lives and speak their own languages. Even the Welsh and the Scots to say nothing of the Irish have small but active cultural uprisings against central authority. The religious equivalents of these things are cults. Protestants and Catholics tend to be cerebral at the top, but in the villages are the cults of Saints and the cults of little groups. There are even people who see Elvis Presley walking around. A cult is not just a bunch of crazy people in the formal sense. A cult is a religious group trying to express the reality behind the text, trying to get beyond the cerebral and develop a close, intimate, hands-on religion. A cult is of time and place and involves folk piety as well as the formal teachings. Cult is body and heart, whereas we tend to expect religion to be mind and soul. Saints, for instance, are friends and helpers, protectors, ordinary men and women who lived the lives we live and did the things we do. They are our brothers and sisters. They show us all the shapes and forms of life in its day-to-dayness and how we might live. They interpret the meaning and majesty of God in the here and now. They bring the meaning of life into our life.

The ecology movement is a something of a cult. The ecology movement is not sparked by people who sit about and cerebrate so much as it is people who experience nature and see in the particularity that whale, this wilderness, this lake, the air we breathe today an image of the whole. This past week there was a TV news story about 3 whales trapped in the ice pack in the arctic and how rescue seemed impossible. The people doing the news made sympathetic and personal statements after the formal text. Twenty years ago that probably would not even have been reported. But when it becomes close and personal, as this story did, you are moving toward cult experience. Not just whales, but trapped whales and we have sympathy for them instead of seeing them as steaks or dog food or burgers or a source of fats and oils. Not an abstraction of wild life ought to be preserved either, but those three whales ought to be helped. This edges us into the cult experience.

There are alternatives. The Taoists comprehended systems theory thousands of years ago and teach now, as they taught then, that everything is interconnected, each life is an expression of the one life, each thing is part of the totality. We are no more nor less part of that life and totality than the rocks and the trees and the water, and we need the beasts of the field as much as we need each other. As modern ecologists point out, we haven't much chance of living in a world unfit for animal life.

The reading from Exodus reminds us that in our religious history there have been those times when we recognized that to be whole and holy we needed the cult object, the unhewn stone, the place of wilderness, the place close to the earth and nature.

Wes Jackson, picks up on that theme in his book "Altars of Unhewn Stone" (Jackson, 1987) which is about agricultural policy and experimental work with ecologically sound farming Jackson writes: (p. 91) "we do need a future we can affirm. We do need a future that is neither so hopeful as to be unrealistic, nor so grim as to invite despair. I don't believe there is a juggernaut of history, for there is plenty of evidence that individual and group actions have had significant consequences. We have it in our power to take the best of the old and promote an attractive and healthful rural landscape. We have in our scientific inventory, particularly in the areas of ecology, population biology, and evolutionary biology, an abundance of scientific knowledge derived from discoveries about ecosystems and how they work. That knowledge can be directed to great use in the development of a sustainable agriculture."

And, we can add, a sustainable world for all of us. If the ecology movement is a cult, part of what we can do is become part of that cult and seek the oneness with life and the world which it offers us.

October, 1988

The Earth as Nigger

We lived in South Africa for three years. It is getting to be a long time ago. We left there in 1971 but the memories are sharp and when we consider treating people like dirt we remember what it was like to be privileged.

There are two incidents I recall of many that describe what it means: In the first some small children, perhaps 10 or 11, were playing in a yard up the street from us. In Vredehoek, the suburb of Cape Town in which we lived, most of the houses had walls around the yard, or garden as we called it there, with a gate leading to the street. Sometimes the walls were quite high, but often, as in this case, no more than 3 or 4 feet high, enough to demarcate the garden, not high enough to spoil the view. The boys were playing with gliders, tossing them into the air and chasing them around the garden. Across the street was a moving van, being offloaded of furniture by a crew of black men. Labor was cheap and crews always went with delivery trucks. We ordered some fireplace coal once, 4 bags, and the truck that delivered it had two black men in the cab and 4 sitting on 6 or 8 bags of coal in the back. In any event the crew was unloading the truck, the boys were playing, the sun was shining, there was a gentle breeze, and it was a lovely day. One of the boys tossed the glider into the air, a breeze caught it and it sailed up over the garden wall, made a graceful flip and came to ground near the van. One of the boys walked over to the wall and yelled at a black men who was lifting a piece of furniture, "Hey you, you, Boy, Yes you," as the black man looked at him, "You boy, pick that up and bring it here." The black man put down the piece of furniture, picked up the glider and carried it to the boy who took it without a word of thanks, and they both went back to what they had been doing.

In the other incident, we were having dinner with out fruit and vegetable man, Mr. Ibrahim, and his family. One of his relatives was a neatly dressed Colored man and I started talking with him. He told me that I didn't belong there, that I didn't understand what was going on, and that if the Colored people (the blacks were probably hopeless) would only behave better they (including him and his family) would not be treated so badly. He thought that the government ought to be more severe in punishment of offenders of any type, to whip them into line so that he and his family would be treated better some day.

I think that these incidents are good examples of what being treated like dirt, being treated, as Alice Walker so sharply puts it, as niggers, does to us. And the worst part is that we come to accept it. Why did not the moving man tell the boy to pick it up himself? Why did the Colored man believe that he deserved to be treated the way he was? Why do we believe that homeless people deserve their fate, or that AIDS victims should be isolated and ostracized?

There is a school of thought that says we make ourselves feel good be making someone else look bad, that we attain and maintain status by having other people in positions that we perceive as lower than our own. If I want to be top dog, there have to be bottom dogs to snarl at.

I used to walk from Vredehoek to downtown Cape Town. Once in a while, I would wander off the main street to side streets and one day realized that I was walking down a street where there were no gardens, where the front doors opened on the sidewalk, where grubby and often ill looking children played in the gutters, where families were living in houses no larger than some of our living rooms. I asked a friend about the area. I was amazed at seeing whites living in poverty, and was told that the government line with them was that at least they were white, and they accepted that. No matter how poor they were, and they were poor, they were better than any black or Colored simply because they were white.

We have become used to hierarchical thinking; it is part of us. People in positions of power assume that they know best, and we believe them. The New York Times for 7 November 1988, for instance, reported that in the first months of the Reagan administration, a deliberate decision was made not to overhaul safety programs at nuclear weapons plants. Most of the plants are now closed for safety reasons. One estimate tells us that it will take $ 180 Billion to clean up the radioactive waste that has been strewn across the state of Ohio in a deliberate decision to run the nuclear weapons facility in spite of the problems. That is hierarchical thinking; we good people in the government know what is best for you and you should not question us. It is, in essence, treating all of us as niggers.

Alice Walker (Walker, 1988) tells us earth is being treated as a nigger. We don't have to go very far to see this attitude expressed. The walkway from the library to the school and to the Superette is a trail of trash, soda cans, potato chip bags, candy wrappers, and other garbage. We are part of that earth and when the earth is treated as nigger, we are also. What happens to the earth happens to us. When we denigrate the ground upon which we walk, we denigrate our friends, our neighbors, and eventually, ourselves.

But it is not all gloom and doom. I think that the whales of Alaska are a hopeful sign. People have been very critical of the effort to save first three and then two whales. After about a week of human interest stuff, we suddenly heard the TV people talking about what it cost and began to discuss priorities. A worthy discussion, as the Rev. Barbara Merritt of the First Unitarian Church in Worcester points out in a recent newsletter; "Some social activists wrung their hands that so much attention and money was 'wasted' on three (and then two) whales, when people are hungry and homeless all over the world. But an act of compassion towards a few members of an endangered species does not take resources away from needy human beings. One can show kindness towards animals and people. If you're really upset about priorities, then figure out how much money is spent on pets, entertainment, foolish luxuries, outmoded defense systems, drug trafficking, graft, fine furniture and gourmet food, in comparison with how much we Americans give in charity to either homo sapiens or any other life form. Compare and weep."

And, she concludes, "....All of us know what it feels like to be trapped. All of us are trapped in our lives to one degree or another. We have sometimes felt our world closing in on us, and we have also hoped and prayed for a pathway to freedom. When those two surviving whales made it to the open sea, I believe that a part of every one of us who indentified with those creatures felt a breath of freedom for ourselves. Those whales have given humanity one more image of what it means to hang on, to persist and to rise above impossible odds (with a lot of help) and continue on our long journey home."

More than knowing what it feels like to be trapped, we also all know what it is like to be treated as nigger to be treated like dirt, to have our dignity demeaned. To be considered nothing except as we are useful to someone else. I agree with the Rev. Mrs. Merritt, the whales gave us a good image, and it gave us an example of what can be done when people (including Russians) work together to a common end. I think the whales tapped the depths of human compassion, became a symbol of individuals caught and in need of help. I think the whole incident reminded us that we could care, that we could show compassion. I think some real leadership would tap that care and compassion and make our country a better place for everyone, including the earth itself.

You and I need to take responsibility for how our bit of the world is treated, how we treat the earth, what our priorities are, whether or not we get good feelings off the denigrating of others, whether or not we care.

November, 1988

On Being Shrunk

I have a text from W. H. Auden:

We would rather be ruined than changed.
We would rather die in our dread
Than climb the cross of the moment
And let our illusions die

and a text from Alfred Korsybski:

God may forgive your sins,
but your nervous system won't.

We live in a world of numberless options, it sometimes seems, often described by that wretched term "lifestyle."

Newspapers have lifestyle editors, and stores hire lifestyle consultants. Some years ago the bank we were using started lifestyle banking which got us so annoyed that we took the opportunity to open a checking account with a credit union where Trudi was working. When I go into a bank I want to discuss money, not my lifestyle.

We live in a world where much of our input about what is and what is not going on, what is and what is not the way people should behave, what is and what is not the way we ought to feel, comes from people whose primary concern is to make money by entertaining us, to entertain us in order to extract money from us. A real growth industry right now is plastic surgery: the "sculpting" and reshaping our bodies to meet some fantasy about perfection in our appearance.

We are bombarded with books and magazines and newspaper articles and talk show guests telling us how to make our lives perfect, through everything from raising our children to improving our sex lives along with surgical alterations to everything from head to toe. I get tempted sometimes; I do wonder what I would look like with well articulated abs and maybe a bit taller, but then I decide that it is too late and so they miss a sale.

Some years back when our children were young, someone came out with a book telling all of us anxious parents how to raise our children properly, but, if we hadn't read their book and done what they said before the children were 5 it was too late and their lives were ruined. Our youngest was 7 at the time so I decided her life was already ruined and didn't bother to look for the book in the library, much less consider buying it.

We want freedom from the limits that life puts on us, whether those limits are political, economic, or biological, our appearance, or our own emotional make-up. We live in a paradox: On the one hand we are under constant pressure to conform to the media images of beauty and success; on the other hand we function without the community standards and sanctions and controls which we used to have to form and shape our behavior. In many ways this can be wonderful. We end up with some highly creative people and we end up with people doing exciting things. But we may also end up very much "at sea," to use an old expression that is drifting rather aimlessly along. Or we may up in crisis situations with nowhere to turn. We each live a life story. There is strong evidence that family patterns can be passed from generation to generation. Child abusers tend to have been abused as children. Adult children of alcoholics follow dependency and rescuing patterns typical of alcoholics and their families.

We all know how difficult it is to change our behavior. Trudi and I still remember, discuss now and then, the difficulties we went through when we decided to quit smoking. Or consider the number of times my physician has told me to lose weight.

We tend to think of living in terms of events. We measure our lives by events, graduations, getting a job, getting married, having children, choosing a career, learning a skill, buying a home. My favorite rant and rave is the wedding. I like weddings, they are fun, and it is lovely to see a couple join their lives. I been involved in weddings for many couples, some very young and even had one absolutely wonderful one for a couple in their late eighties. What I rant and rave about, not at weddings however, are the people who want us to believe that a wedding is "the happiest day of my/your/our/his/her life." A wedding is a happy day, but we have to hope that life isn't all downhill from there.

We need to remind ourselves, life is a process, not an event. Events are punctuation marks in the story of our life, and not the whole story.

Being married, being in a marriage, is not an event, it is a process. If I could give what I think is good advice to all of the people getting married, and all the people who are married, and all the people who are in any long term relationship, it would be that relationships are not events, they are processes. A relationship is a day-to-day, year-to-year, process of growth and relationship and change. A relationship is not something that happens, it is something to be involved in. Theodore Parker, a 19th Century Unitarian (Dirks, 1970), described marriage as "a long falling in love."

Someone once made a remark to the effect that in life we intend to tell one story and our great awakening comes when we realize that we are telling a totally different one. Which brings me to therapy! Hence my title today, *On Being Shrunk,* based on the slang expression of "shrink" to describe a psychiatrist or psychologist. And, I think, we are "shrunk" when any source of life enhancing change occurs for us.

Viktor Frankl, a psychiatrist from Vienna who survived the WWII death camps (Frankl, 1946) said that he learned in that experience that the question is not "what is the meaning of life?", but "what is the meaning of my life?" A small, but for him and many others, a significant and life changing difference. The big questions are intellectual and theological fun. But Frankl decided that they did little for him in the day-to-day struggle to stay alive. "What is the meaning of my life here and now." How do I live "today, this hour, this minute" became his guide. And, ultimately, he decided, he could even die with dignity if it came to that.

Dr. Phil, of TV fame, may not be our favorite source of insight into life, but he has a question he likes to ask which I think is worth considering, "Would you rather be right or be happy?" I think for many of us the answer is "I would rather be right," when what we really want is happiness. To find happiness we may have to change our behavior.

Jesus told his followers that they must be born again. The message is at the heart of much of our religious teaching, we must be born again, to find renewal and growth. Jesus' disciples fell to quarreling one day as to which one of them was to be the greatest in the coming kingdom and Jesus settled the argument by having a child come and stand with them and saying "Whosoever would be great among you, let him be as this child." How is a child? Fresh, open to newness, learning, willing to explore the world and life, not burdened down with assumptions and baggage from the past. Not perfect, but growing. One of our Unitarian Universalist ministers has picked up on this and said "We must be born again and again and again." We want an instant cure don't we? A pill, an injection, an implant, a winning lottery ticket … and we will be happy. Earl Holt III, minister of King's Chapel in Boston differentiates between curing and healing: a cure is a fix as in an antibiotic will cure certain infections. Healing is more a Viktor Frankl thing – how do I make the best of my life here and now? What do I do to give my life meaning even if I can't 'fix' the circumstances? How do I manage my problems instead of my problems managing me? Curing is an event, healing is a process under this definition. A good therapist will help us learn to manage our psychological life. A useful religion will help us learn to manage our spiritual life. Finally, as my dentist says, "Speaking as your friend, take care of yourself."

April, 1988, Adapted November, 2005

Belfort, New York, The Place Of My Dreams

My heart's in the Highlands, my heart is not here,
My heart's in the Highlands a-chasing the deer
... Robert Burns

Belfort, New York, is the place of my dreams. I was born there in 1932, left at the age of seven, returned for three years at the age of sixteen and moved away in 1951. I have made occasional visits since. In German, I read somewhere, there is the word *heimweh,* meaning "homesickness," or "home-ache," but more than that, it is nostalgia and the pain of knowing that we cannot go home. As in Thomas Wolfe's *You Can't Go Home Again.* I go back there but most of the people I knew are gone, some of them I don't know where. One of my friends, rumor had it, a bachelor, to the end of his life, had a pack of dogs and lived in squalor in a shack. It was so filthy that after they found him dead all of his dogs were shot and the shack, condemned by the health department, was burned by the volunteer fire department. "Sorry about Wilbur," I said to my sister as we drove down the road he had lived on. "Oh," she said, "He did all right. Built a nice house – there, that one – and was pretty healthy up to the end." "What about all the dogs they had to shoot?" I asked. "What dogs?" she replied. It was a nice house. So much for rumor.

Wilbur's parents ran Lambert's Country Store in Belfort, New York. The Belfort of my memory, located about six miles outside of the Adirondack State Park, consisted of a district school, the Nortz House (later the Belfort Inn), St. Vincent de Paul Catholic Church, a grange hall (Grange P of H 533), several private dwellings, and a dam and hydroelectric plant. The Beaver River drops down out of the Adirondacks and runs by Belfort. In 1899 the first of a series of eight hydroelectric plants was opened there. The plant supplied electricity to Lowville, New York, 14 miles away over what was, at the time, the longest electrical transmission line in the world. My father told the story of the man who appeared at the power plant one day with horse and buggy, walked down the path and steps to the plant and greeted the operator. "This were they make the 'lectricity stuff?" "It is." "I hear tell its better'n kerosene fer light." "'Tis." "Got me a couple clean kerosene cans in the buggy, could I have them filled? I'd like to try it this winter."

My father, born in 1910, went to the country school. His family spoke German, he learned English in school. My mother, born in 1912, was also a student there. My three brothers and sister started school there as did I. In the late 1940s country schools were being closed and students bussed to a central school. There was a school halfway between our house and Croghan that remained open longer than any other. Most of the students came from two nearby farms where there were 17 or 18 children and the farmers flatly refused to allow them to go on the bus.

Lambert's Store was kitty-corner across the street, 50 yards or so from the Belfort school. The store was two stories with a concrete pad across the front, one step up from the road. A porch ran across the second floor front. There was a Gulf gas pump out front and the building was painted white with Gulf blue and Gulf orange trim. Someone in the family had planted a lemon seed in a pot and it had grown big enough to eventually end up in a 55 gallon drum, also painted blue and orange. The tree sat on the concrete pad in the summer and was moved inside for the winter.

Clara and Walter Lambert (Clara was always named first) had living quarters in the store and raised two sons and a daughter there. Clara ran the store and Walter worked for the power company, had a "sugar bush," did some hunting and fishing. Walter was slightly built, five feet five at the most, and my memory of him is that he always wore suspenders to hold up pants that must have been four to six inches too large around the waist. Clara was no taller but much, much heavier. Next door was the Peters' store, a similar operation with the Peters family living there. They also had a gas pump, Esso I think.

Our house is roughly half-a-mile from Belfort as the crow flies, not as much as twice that as the horse trots. We have to cross two bridges to go from our house to Belfort center, the first over a gorge cut into bedrock by the river, as much as a 50 foot drop from the bridge to the rock and water below. Right under the bridge is a wonderful kettle-hole worn into the rock by centuries of rushing water. The second bridge, 50 yards further on, spans the water inlet for the power plant. In recent years a canoe portage has been built around the dam but when I was growing up there was no such thing.

Both stores sold candy and Peters' sold ice cream on a stick and popsickles in the summer. I remember going to the store with my older brother Norman, I was next, then David. Howard and Betty not yet born. For our nickel we got a Three Musketeers bar. We tore open the wrapping and there were three miniature bars, one for each of us, chocolate covered fondue, one chocolate, one vanilla, and one strawberry. The stores stocked canned goods, bread, a few baked goods, flour, sugar, condiments, tobacco products, soaps, odds and ends. Peters' sold ammunition and hunting and fishing supplies including some bright red and black plaid jackets (before the days of

Shooter's Orange). Lambert's sold maple syrup from their sugar bush, and Clara kept bees and sold some honey. Rumor was that when she cleaned the penny candy counter she put the stale candy where the bees could get to it. One year the bees got into cinnamon hearts and produced pinkish honey with a tinge of cinnamon flavor.

There was an old man living three or four miles from Belfort named Jakie Kohler. Jakie would show up at Lambert's with a burlap bag and buy groceries: Several loaves of bread, six or eight cans of sweetened condensed milk for coffee, canned corned beef and Spam, sardines, salt and sugar as needed, coffee, odds and ends. With everything paid for and laid out on the counter, he proceeded to open his sack and drop his purchases in by size, bread first followed by canned goods. Throwing the sack over his shoulder he walked home. Leaving Clara and others to wonder what the bread looked like when he got there.

Peters' sold frozen confections – popsicles, Eskimo pies, and real ice cream cones.

Walter Lambert died in 1975. One of the provisions of his will was that the building was to be burned – practice for the volunteer fire department. The fate of several buildings in the area.

My parent's home was next to Gospel Hall. There was a cemetery laid out around a clapboard church built on land acquired for that purpose in 1890. Built on pilings, the hall was gradually sinking into the ground. There was no official denominational affiliation. There was the occasional funeral, church services if a nearby minister was willing to preach for the collection – not much from a gathering of fewer than a dozen. It is where my parents are buried. The Lamberts were the surviving trustees of the Gospel Hall and, unable to raise money for necessary repairs, offered it to the volunteer fire department for practice. The Grange Hall met the same fate.

Lambert's General Store was spared. The fire chief declared it too close to other buildings and it was torn down instead. One theory is that Walter wanted the building burned to hide the evidence. When the cellar was emptied out, a pile of boxes, crates, and old furniture was dragged out to reveal said evidence. A still was discovered along with a stock of gallon jugs hidden behind all the detritus. The still was vented through the chimney. Speculation was that the store would have been a perfect front for ordering sugar, yeast, grain, and other supplies. The store had done well during the Depression according to old timers. Better than people expected, so the gossip goes, and the still would help explain the apparent prosperity of the family.

Walter had an automobile, but his favorite vehicle was a 1928 Willys Overland delivery wagon. A tall machine with wood spoke wheels useful for hauling wood and supplies. It was his vehicle for taking supplies up to his sugar bush and bringing out the maple syrup in drums.

The Nortz House, the local bar, started as a hotel of which little is known except that the original had burned to be replaced in 1875 by a hotel with a ball room, dining facilities, rooms for the owners, and nine rooms upstairs. In 1977 the top floor was taken off. People such as my father and his brother, Uncle Benny, "pissed away a fortune" as one of my brothers describes it, in the Nortz House. It has since been renamed The Belfort Inn. Trudi and I decided, a few years back, to stop there on one of our visits. We walked in about 10 in the morning and the woman behind the bar waved us to a table. There were four or five men at the bar, with beer, and they gave us puzzled looks, whispered a bit, and went back to drinking. The bar tender came to the table and asked us what we wanted. "Coffee" we replied. "Oh," she said, "I can make some." "It's alright," we said, "We don't. . . ." "No, no," she insisted, "I can make it." Returning to the bar she said something and we got another round of stares and mutters. I swear I recognized a couple of the men that they had been there since the 1940s. Maybe there were family resemblances.

Belfort had been quite prosperous at one time, even had its own post office. In the 1860s a tannery was built supplied with hides shipped in from South America eventually arriving in Belfort by mule train. The tanning was made possible by hemlock forest around Belfort. The trees were cut and the bark stripped and stacked, the logs being left to rot. The bark was hauled to the tannery where it was chopped, leached and the liquor put in tubs where the hides were soaked. In 1894, the supply of bark reaching exhaustion, the tannery was closed. Irish immigrant families who had settled there to work in the tannery wandered off. A young man named Theodore Basselin (1851-1914) from nearby Croghan, just home from college, decided that leaving the logs to rot was a waste and began hiring crews to gather the logs and float them down the river to a sawmill. By the time he died, he was a millionaire (roughly $20,000,000 in 2007 purchasing value).

My father's family was not wealthy, though they did prosper as farmers. They were Amish/Mennonites, German speaking Alsatians who immigrated to Lewis County in northern New York starting in 1832.

My father was born in 1910 and was something of a "rake-hell." Had a drinking problem all of his life; not a steady drunk, nor a mean one, but a binge drinker. He would stop at a bar anytime he had money, such as his paycheck, and celebrate. Our mother often had to deal with him coming home late on pay day with all of his money gone. He farmed for a time for my grandmother Widrick after he was first married. Some of my earliest memories are of me on the farm walking behind my father as he plowed with a team of horses and me with a tin can picking up worms. Attached is the memory of a bucket kept in the cellar filled with earth where the worms were kept until they were needed for fishing. I want to say that Dad would sometimes sprinkle corn meal in the bucket to feed the worms. His name was Ruben, though sometimes spelt Reuben. Most people called him Rudy. There seemed to have been some intention to name him Rudolph and the doctor who delivered him may have filled out the birth certificate wrongly. He was the youngest of eight children, one of whom had died in adolescence. His father, Daniel, was a tall man, much in contrast to his mother Fannie who was short. Daniel and Fannie were married in November 1897. They lived on the family farm all their lives, Daniel dying in 1933 age 57. Fannie lived until 1970, age 93. My father died at Christmas time in 1956, and I remember her standing by his grave saying that it was not fair, children were supposed to bury their parents and she had already buried children.

Daniel would buy a wagon load of grapes every fall from a peddler and make wine in barrels in the cellar. He had a drinking problem, according to the family memories, and would go to church and kneel before the pulpit praying to be freed of his sin. The congregation would pray for him, the ministers would lay hands on him, and he would go home, go down cellar and begin drinking. My father told of Fannie sitting by Daniel's bed as he died and, when he breathed his last, covering his face with the sheet and going down cellar to knock the bungs out of his barrels, saving one gallon for "medicinal purposes." The cellar had a dirt floor and my father remembered the smell permeating the house for a year. The "medicinal wine" went to Uncle Benny for his wife who was dying of Tuberculosis.

Uncle Benny was a woodsman. He made a business during WW II of providing venison for people without the necessity of using meat ration coupons. After my grandmother died Uncle Benny woke up one morning and found that he was no longer thirsty. He went and got a job at what had been a CCC camp, taken over by 4H, where there was a program to teach woodcraft, hunting, and the skills of foresters. He mentored a generation of youths and was so well liked and admired that they named the administration building after him.

Rudy, my father, had a Ford runabout as a teen. Model T two-seater. About the only thing I clearly remember him saying about the car was that he could outrun anything the State Police could put on the road in that part of the world and they never caught him.

My parents left school as soon as the law allowed which I think was age 14 in their day. My mother left to work as a domestic with a farm family, my father left to work on the farm. My mother, Leona, did well in school and had tried to convince her parents to allow her to go to high school. The custom was for children to quit school and go to work. Their parents expected that they would collect the wages – really generous parents would allow the children to keep half their pay. Usually until the child was 18, sometimes even 21.

The Widrick side of the family was rather strict about photographs. Grandma Widrick would get angry if you even pointed a camera in her direction. There are a few pictures: She was very short, Daniel was over six feet tall. There is a picture of my father as a teenager with his pet bull. A large animal, he had managed to train it, got along well with it, and when it came time, late afternoon, to bring in the cows for milking he would get out the bull, tie a rope to the ring in its nose, mount up, and ride the bull off to the roundup.

My father worked the family farm for my grandmother for a time. I remember living there with my parents and my older brother Norman and younger brother David. My grandmother lived there and my aunt Esther. There was the day that I became aware that people could do something I later learned was called "counting." I went into the kitchen and saw a mesh basket of eggs sitting on the counter by the sink. I had a mud-pie project out behind the barn and thought that a few eggs would improve the mix inasmuch as eggs were used in cakes and other things. I filled my pockets and went off to my "bakery" and was much pleased with the results of the egg and mud recipe. I returned to the house and was asked what I had done with the eggs. I lied, proclaimed my innocence. But they knew that eggs were missing, I was punished, and I "knew" that there was some way of knowing the eggs were gone.

My Mother, Leona Marolf, started life on a farm a couple of miles down the road towards Croghan. At some point, I don't know when, her parents moved to Carthage, NY, where her father Edward took a job in a feed mill. Her Mother Ida was a housewife. They had three children, Mom, Aunt Ruthie, and a son who died in his teens.

I must have been about five or six when our parents bought a house and we moved there. We were located next to Gospel Hall on Belfort Road, running from Belfort about four or five miles to Croghan. The road ran along a plateau which dropped away to a stretch of flat land and the river. Our house was about a hundred yards from where the land began to drop.

My father did various things to make a living: Worked for my grandmother, was a lumberjack, sometimes a cook in a lumber camp (he was a good cook), worked off and on in paper mills (he hated the regular hours he was expected to keep) and during hunting season worked at hunting camps as a guide. I met an orthopedic surgeon in Syracuse, NY, who knew him from hunting camp, and about 1989 ran into a parishioner in Auburn, NY, who had his father with him who recognized the name from the same hunting camp. His last job was working for his brother, my uncle Daniel. Dannie had a farm and ran a butcher shop. Slaughtered animals, sold meat retail, butchered for other people, cured hams and bacon and made sausages of various types. One bright morning in October 1956 my father left home headed for Dannie's. A neighbor working near the road waved at him as he drove by. Rudy liked to sing as he drove; it was a warm day so he had the car window down. The neighbor recalled him singing the familiar words, "When the trumpet of the Lord shall sound, and time shall be more, / And the morning breaks, eternal, bright and fair; / When the saved of earth shall gather over on the other shore, / And the roll is called up yonder, I'll be there. . . ." fading away in the distance. He got to work, went out to the smoke house to boil rings of bologna preparatory to smoking them. He was careless with fire. I remember him burning trash at home in a barrel, lighting fires in the wood stove, burning brush piles. If the fire did not perform the way he wanted it to he would douse it with kerosene and grin as the fire exploded. The smoke house fire must have been too slow for him; he picked up a gallon can, the old metal kind with a screw top and a spout on the side. It was used to carry kerosene and old crank case oil for fires. Later it was thought, though no one would admit it, that someone had carried gasoline in the can. He apparently threw some of the contents on the fire, the stream burst into flame, the can exploded, blowing open about a third of the bottom seam so that several quarts of flaming kerosene and oil, and evidently some gas, blew out toward him and caught him in the stomach. He ran for help struggling to tear off his clothing. Dannie knocked him down and rolled him on the ground. Bishop Lloyd Boshart of the Mennonite church drove in, went over and knelt beside him. My father spoke with him in German, spoke little English again. Boshart accompanied him to the hospital. As soon as they had him stabilized he was transferred to the University Hospital in Syracuse, New York. Massive third, fourth, fifth and even sixth degree burns with places on his right arm and hands where the flesh was burned away to the bone. The hospital staff fought a valiant but losing battle. Rudy had his legs wrapped in bandages with little tubes sticking out into which they injected something to keep the raw flesh moist. A few small skin grafts were attempted but he hadn't a lot of skin to get the grafts from. Shortly before he died the hospital had us sign papers volunteering to donate skin grafts if our blood types matched. Apparently not much hope of long term success but they were trying to buy time to let his body heal as much as it could. Being a woodsman Rudy was aware that girdling a tree would kill it. In a period of lucidity he asked Leona to check under his bandages and his back to find out if he had been "girdled." He had not, to his great relief. And being a man, he asked her one day to check under the covers to make certain that his "private parts" had not been lost (he was catheterized so unaware of urine passing). He died the 20th of December.

Rudy was laid out in our living room and that is where the funeral service was held, conducted by his brother in law, Elias Zehr, a Bishop of the Mennonite church. The bishop was a kind and remarkable man. Rudy was buried next door to our home in the Gospel Hall Cemetery.

"Tuffy" Dicoup (pronounced 'Dee Cup'), who had worked in the woods with Rudy, guided with him, and spent a lot of time drinking with him, came to the calling hours and he and I talked into the night about the woods and hunting and friendship. We provided coffee; Tuffy provided his own pint of brandy. One of Rudy's favorite stories was about Tuffy. Tuffy had shot a deer, in season which was a bit unusual for him, but without antlers. As he was hauling the deer down a logging road a game warden stepped out and demanded to see his hunting license and then, looking at the deer said, "That's not a buck." "Got balls ain't it?" Tuffy replied and hauled the deer off. Tuffy told me a story I had never heard, how he and Rudy were guiding at a hunting camp one autumn. Late in the afternoon – late in the sense that the sun was low in the sky – they had most of the men back at the camp putting away rifles and ammunition when they heard shots. The two of them started off towards the shots to meet one of their hunters. "We heard shots." "Yeah, I think I hit a bear." "Where the hell is it?" "Ran off into brush." "Get back to camp" Rudy grumbled. The two of them had followed his trail until they smelled gunpowder, found clots of blood on some bushes, then they trailed the wounded beast into some swampy area. A sudden roar and the bear reared up in front of them. "Stand behind me," Rudy said, "and be ready to shoot." Then he stepped forward, held his rifle at waist height and fired. The bear lunged forward and Rudy fired off all five rounds in his rifle, the bear pitched forward and slashed with a paw. Dead, his claws, according to Tuffy, were less than half an inch from the tip of Rudy's boot. Back at the camp Rudy walked up to the man who had wounded the bear: "You can't leave a wounded animal like that, and, dammit, not a wounded bear. It could kill somebody. You get your gear packed and you get the hell out of this camp tomorrow at dawn, and don't you ever let me see your face around here again."

As Tuffy got ready to leave he drew me out onto the back porch and said "You tell your ma I got me a couple a deer hanging in the woods and she can have all the venison she wants."

We buried Rudy December 23, leaving Christmas always a sad time in my memory.

My mother was a good cook though she tended to fry things. To cook bacon she heated a frying pan, threw in a gob of lard, and, when it was hot enough, put in the bacon. But her cakes and pies were excellent and she was fast and efficient. She canned massive amounts of food such as corn, beans, peas, carrots, meat, pickles, jams and jellies. I still crave pickled beets with a few cloves in the jar. Or dilly beans. She died in June 1971 following gall bladder surgery. When we cleaned out the house – my brother Howard had decided to buy it and we were dividing up the contents – we found jars of jams and jellies on the cellar shelves so old that the sugar had crystallized. And quart jars of blackberries she had put up in 1948; the solids had separated from the liquids and settled to the bottoms of the jars, but the jars were still sealed.

My mother had been in the hospital in the Fall of 1950 for several weeks and my father decided to make dill pickles. He sometimes experimented, as in the case of the year when he trapped beaver and decided that beaver burgers would be yummy (they are not, tasted bitter from the bark they ate). We went out in the garden and found some horse-radish growing near a fence, something we never used. But we dug up some roots and dad put a spear of horse-radish in each of about two dozen jars of dill pickles. Mom never forgave him. The rest of us liked them.

Home is still dark clothing, and women with bonnets, men without neckties. A way of life. A pretty woman, to me, is one without make-up. A simple life we claimed, though no life is simple. Just that we did not do much "just for pretty" as my Aunt Ester (Rudy's sister) would say. Or, truth to tell, avoided admitting that it was "just for pretty."

The first cars in the Mennonite community were black, with black paint on all of the chrome work and no radios. Electricity had come early to the area by way of the Belfort Power Plant, and didn't seem to be a problem, though in the 1950's some Mennonites got involved in a more conservative movement and had their electric service disconnected. Their objection was not to electricity but to being billed for the electricity. They wanted cash and carry, not carry and cash.

One of my favorite paintings is the Dali one titled The Persistence of Memory. One of Dali's fantastic landscapes with clocks and watches, but the clocks and watches are fluid, always look to me like eggs as they pour out of the shell, running off the edge of a table, draped over a branch. Time flows and distorts. How much of what I recall is true sixty years and more later? I remember the measles when we had to stay in a room with the shades drawn because the light might hurt our eyes. I remember my brother making mashed potato sandwiches, which were two slices of white bread, a layer of potato, and some mayonnaise. I remember that we found some axel grease, played with it, and tried to clean our hands by wiping them on the clapboards of the house. We got spanked. I remember being in my Grandparent's kitchen, (Mother's side of the family), and a man wearing an army uniform coming to visit. He let me play with his hat and it had a celluloid panel sewn into the crown and he was showing my Grandfather pictures of himself in what I was to later learn was a French Foreign Legion uniform. My aunt who was still at home told me when I asked a few years ago that the visit never happened. I remember that I liked to bite the bottom off of ice cream cones so that the melted ice cream would run out into my mouth and then getting yelled at because the cone dripped. And the day my Father came home with a box of groceries and my Mother looked in the box and said "Where are they," "What?" he asked. "My cigarettes" she replied and they yelled at each other for a while. Grown up I was in the process of quitting smoking and I mentioned it to her and how she could appreciate how difficult it was. "I never smoked," she said. "Yes, you did." "No, I never did." Another liquid Dali watch dripping off a window sill.

The American humorist and cartoonist James Thurber (1894-1961) is quoted as having described love as "what we have been through together." "Love is what we have been through together." What we have been through. Together! I don't suppose our memories have to be all that accurate, time has flowed. This is what we have been through together.

A bit of mythology that I need to check the next time I am home: I have it set in my mind that the Old Order Amish Church in Croghan, NY, that my Grandparents belonged to buries people by date. Behind the church is the burying ground with rows and rows of small markers. There are no family plots. Everyone is buried in turn, which would leave my grandparents buried 37 years apart. Seems rather nice, noting the separation of time, the years that passed without each other, honoring the flow of time. I decided one day that if I moved back there and went to the church elders and apologized for leaving they might let me have a space when my time comes. But I don't even know if the burial arrangement is what I think it is, and, as old Tom Wolfe so aptly put if "You can't go home again."

But we went through our lives together if only for a time, and that is the essence and the presence of love.

May, 2010

Bibliography

AUUA. (1937). *Hymns of the Spirit, Universalist Church in America.* Boston: American Unitarian Association.

Ballou, R. O. (1948). *The Pocket World Bible.* Routledge & Kegan.

Berne, E. (1964). *Games People Play: The Psychology of Human Relationships.* New York: Ballantine Books.

Bierce, A. (1899). Works by Ambrose Bierce: Fantastic Fables. New York: Putnam.

Boerstler, R. W. (1982). *Letting Go: A Holistic and Meditative Approach to Living and Dying.* Associates in Thanatology.

Bond, M. (2003). World Values Survey. *New Scientist Magazine*.

Christ, C. P. (1980). *Diving Deep and Surfacing.* New York: Beacon Press.

Church, F. (2000). *Lifecraft: The Art of Meaning in the Everyday.* Boston: Beacon Press.

Churchill, W. S. (2003). *Never Give In! The Best of Winston Churchill's Speeches.* Great Britain: Random House.

Cummings, C. (1989). Exploring Eco-Spirituality. *Spirituality Today, 41* (1), 35.

Cunningham, L. S. (1978). The Pursuit of Marginality. *Christian Century*, 1181-1183.

Davies, W. H. (1911). *Songs of Joy and Others.* Fifield.

Davis, B. (1997). Marginality in a Pluralistic Society. *Eye on Psi Chi*, Vol. 2, iss. 1.

Davis, W. V. (2007). *R.S. Thomas, Poetry and Theology.* Waco: Baylor University Press.

Dirks, J. E. (1970). *DirThe Critical Theology of Theodore Parker.* New York: Columbia University Press.

Enslin, M. S. (1938). *Christian Beginnings.* New York: Book by Morton Scott Enslin; Harper & Brothers, 1938..

Enslin, M. S. (1961). *The Prophet from Nazareth.* New York: McGraw Hill.

Foote II, A. (Ed.). (1964). *Hymns for the Celebration of Life : A Unitarian Universalist Hymnal.* Boston: Beacon Press.

Frankl, V. E. (1946). *Man's Search For Meaning: An Introduction to Logotherapy .* Boston: Beacon Press .

Globe-Staff. (2000, November 22). Underage of consent. *Boston Globe* , p. Living Arts Section.

Goldberg, C. (2008, March). Money Pays More If You Give It Away. *Boston Globe .*

Graham, A. (1974). Syntactic Differences Between Speech and Writing. *New York Times* , 46.

Green, H. (2000). *Saint Foy, Little Saint.* New York: Random House.

Hall, A. (1951). *James Martineau Selections .* Boston: Beacon Press.

Hanh, T. N. (1988). The Individual, Society, and Nature. In F. Eppsteiner, *The Path of Compassion, Writings on Socially Engaged Budhism* (p. 40). New York: Parallax Press.

Harris, M. (1995). *Jubiliee Time.* Bantam Books.

Heller, E. (1995). *Doctor of Philosophy Dissertation of South African Unitarians.* Cambridge: Copy in Harvard Divinity School Library.

Herbermann, C. G. (1913). *Mechtild of Magdeburga.* New York: Robert Appleton Company.

Hopkins, G. M. (1918). *Poems of Gerard Manley Hopkins .* London: Humphrey Milford.

Housman, A. E. (1896). *A Shropshire Lad.* London.

Isaacs, W. (1999). *Dialogue and the Art of Thinking Together .* New York: Doubleday.

Jackson, W. (1987). *Altars of Unhewn Stone: Science and the Earth.* New York: North Point Press.

Jantzen, G. (1988). *Julian of Norwich : Mystic and Theologian.* Paulist Press.

Lear, M. W. (1975). Mother's Day: Bitter- sweet. *New York Times* , 13.

Marcuse, H. (2000). *Martin Niemöller's Famous Quotation.* Santa Barbara: UC Santa Barbara.

McCullers, C. (1946). *The Member of the Wedding.* New York: Houghton Mifflin Company.

Moore, T. (1994). *Care of the Soul : A Guide for Cultivating Depth and Sacredness in Everyday Life* . New York: HarperPerennial.

Nichols, R. J. (2000). The Story of Creation in the Jewish scriptures. *Unitarian Universalist Society of Wellesley Hills Newsletter* .

Nissenbaum, S. (1997). *The Battle for Christmas.* New York: Vintage Books.

Papers, W. L. (1982). *William Laurence Sullivan. Papers, 1895-1961.* Andover: Andover-Harvard Theological Library, Harvard Divinity School.

Park, R. E. (1921). *Race and Culture.* Glencoe, IL: The Free Press.

Peart, A. (2008, April). "Deconsidered by Men." Women and the British Unitarian Movement before 1904. *Transactions of the Unitarian Historical Society* , pp. 61-65.

Plath, S. (1967). *The Colossus and Other Poems.* Faber and Faber.

Roy, B. K. (1977). *Rabindranath Tagore: The Man and His Poetry.* Folcroft Library Editions.

Schweitzer, A. (1910). *The Quest of the Historical Jesus.* London: A. & C. Black, Ltd.

Schweitzer, A. (1965). *The Story of My Pelican.* New York: Hawthorn Books.

Shields, S. K. (1955). *Edwin Markham: A Bibliography.* Staten Island: Wagner College Publications.

Snyder, G. (1988). Budhism and the Possibility of a Planetary Culture. In F. Eppsteiner, *The Path of Compassion, Writings on Socially Engaged Budhism* (p. 82). New York: Parallax Press.

Sölle, D. (1978). *Death by Bread Alone: Texts and Reflections on Religious Experience.* Philadelphia: Fortress Press.

Sölle, D. (1983). *Not Just Yes and Amen:.* Minneapolis: Fortress Press.

Spencer, T. (1948). *Poems.* Boston: Harvard University Press.

Sullivan, W. L. (1944). *Under Orders: The Autobiography of William Laurence Sullivan* . Boston.

Thurber, J. (1996). *Thurber: Writings and Drawings (Library of America)* . New York: Library of America.

Tillich, P. (1955). *The New Being, Sermon Upon Retirement from Union Theological Seminary.* Lacey, Washington: The Words Group.

Vogt, V. O. (1951). *Cult and Culture: A Study of Religion and American Culture.* New York: Macmillan Company.

Walker, A. (1988). *Living By The Word, Selected Essays.* New York: Houghton Mifflin Harcourt.

Wangchhuk, L. (2008). *Facts About Bhutan, The Land of the Thunder Dragon.* Thimphu Bhutan: Absolute Bhutan Books.

Watterson, B. (1995). *The Calvin and Hobbes Tenth Anniversary Book.* Kansas City: Andrews and McMeel.

White, L. J. (1967). The Historical Roots of Our Ecological Crisis. *Science* , 1203 - 1207.

www.ingramcontent.com/pod-product-compliance
Lightning Source LLC
Chambersburg PA
CBHW032019040426
42448CB00006B/661